BODY TYPES

The Enneagram of Essence Types

by Joel Friedlander

Illustrations by Liza Casey

INNER JOURNEY BOOKS / NEW YORK

Joel Friedlander, *publisher*
Post Office Box 552
Yorktown, NY 10598
U.S.A.

For information on Body Type workshops and seminars,
or to request information about special orders,
please contact the publisher.

Second Edition

ISBN 0-936385-25-1
Library of Congress Catalog Card No: 92-74586

10 9 8 7 6 5 4 3 2 1
Manufactured in the United States

Table of Contents

Acknowledgements

Thanks are due to Robert Burton for introducing this system of types both to me and to thousands of other interested students; to Liza Casey for her efforts to translate the types into useful illustrations; to those who kindly took the time to read the first edition and offer suggestions for its improvement; to Andrea Menken for her general assistance in getting this book into print; and to Paul Harvey for his consistent support.

Foreword

Stanley Krippner, Ph.D.

T he study of the human psyche has been a source of endless fascination for psychologists, psychiatrists, philosophers, writers with a variety of qualifications, and—of course—laypeople. The vast panorama of human behaviors, capacities, and activities has compelled each of these commentators to make explicit or implicit typologies for the purposes of description, explanation, and understanding. Enneagram Theory has now joined this distinguished company and, I believe, has made a major contribution.

As a caveat, I am aware that labels can be overly emphasized. "The word is not the territory," especially when dealing with human beings. Classification systems and personality categories often are useful. But if we forget that these categories are merely working hypotheses, and that they do not refer to an absolutely independent reality, then we forfeit any claim to legitimacy and can become instruments of manipulation, especially if we are psychotherapists.

Joel Friedlander has presented Enneagram Theory in a manner that is easy to read and understand without violating the complexity of his topic. A special contribution is his

7

association of the mythical dieties of ancient Greece and Rome, as well as body glands and functions, with the Enneatypes. These imaginative contributions can lead to the research studies that are urgently needed to justify Enneagram Theory as well as the psychotherapeutic applications that can test the theory clinically. In the meantime, *Body Types: The Enneagram of Essence Types* is a provocative updating of a venerable system of personality exploration.

Stanley Krippner, Ph.D. is Distinguished Professor of Psychology, California Institute of Integral Studies, and co-author of *Personal Mythology* and *Dreamworking*.

Preface

I first learned about the seven body types in 1972. At that time my desire for personal growth was very strong, and I had been looking for a group in which I could pursue this desire in a *practical* way. The system of thought that primarily interested me at the time was the very powerful psychological ideas of G.I. Gurdjieff. I had studied this system for several years, but had been frustrated in finding an active group.

Then, near the end of that year, I came in contact with the school known as the Fellowship of Friends, led by Robert Burton. He used the Gurdjieff system as a basis for his own teaching, but added important elements of his own. The thrust of his work was that as we are, we know little about our basic nature, and must first 'wake up' to a new level of awareness before any real work could be done. Almost all teaching and practical work was aimed at achieving this 'relative awakening' as soon as possible. In our normal state of 'sleep,' we were blind to the real truth of our situation, and would be unable to find any lasting meaning in life.

I joined the group and, as part of my orientation to the work that was going on there, was immediately taught about the seven body types. I was assured that this information was *objective*—that is, that anyone who was properly trained would verify that these same types existed, and could be found in the people around one.

Body types did seem to me to be a very complicated system, with planetary names that I just couldn't seem to keep straight. However, when the characteristics of my own type were explained to me, I had the uncomfortable sensation that occurs when you know you've heard something that's true, that you didn't know *consciously,* but knew instead in some pre-conscious way that never rises to the level of awareness.

As I spent time with students in the group, they used each other and the people around us as examples to teach me the types. Every passer-by, every waiter became material for this study, and it was a matter of weeks before the strange names began to fall into place with their appropriate types.

★ ★ ★

I was told that one of the major benefits to be obtained from studying types would be the deeper appreciation of our personal *subjectivity.* When I began to see myself as a type, I would no longer consider my own thoughts, feelings or attitudes as uniquely *mine.* By showing me that I was invariably a member of a particular type, I hoped to see beyond my type, to what was objectively true. And, in fact, over time I did find that this study was the single most practical tool for beginning the work of breaking down the walls of my own habitual life.

I frequently heard those with more experience of types say that it was the most 'practical' body of knowledge about people they had ever encountered. After several months I began to realize that this might well be true. Knowledge of the types began to enter every interaction I had, with myself and with others. Every relationship was open for reinterpretation based on what soon became a surprisingly obvious reality. Having begun to acquire some ability to recognize types, I realized I no longer had to compare a mental list of criteria to the person in front of me, but simply recognized their body itself, or even their 'energy.'

★ ★ ★

One experience I recall vividly from these early years with the system of types took place in a department store. Day-dreaming while riding the 'Up' escalator, I realized I had been looking at the feet of the person on the steps ahead of me. I had recognized the ankles attached to these feet as typically Venusian; a particular fleshiness I had learned to identify. In that instant, for some reason, everything I knew about the Venusian type dropped into my awareness, and I had the uncomfortable sensation of having invaded this person's privacy—of knowing, in a general way, many things about this person that they might be surprised to find out themselves.

I had another experience with types while driving through Southern California. I had been trying to come to grips with my own type, and was startled to realize that my car was, really, a typical *Jovial-Lunar* car. It was pale, quiet and slightly rounded. I twisted in my seat uncomfortably, but noticed what I was wearing, and how it suddenly seemed just as *Jovial-Lunar* as my car. I began to take a mental inventory of my possessions, and they all seemed to have this same quality. The space in the car was growing warmer, smaller. I thought of my friends, my career choices, and everything whispered *Jovial-Lunar*. For a few moments, I could not imagine doing anything, buying anything, saying anything that was not an expression of my body type. And although I stepped back later, and realized there was more to the story, that we all do contain every type and its possibilities, the vision I had had of being trapped in a particular kind of human 'machine' never left me.

Over the years the *energy* or *theme* behind each type has gone deeper and deeper into my own practice, and I now think *about* the types very little; they have become simply a part of life, an instinctive knowledge deep in the body. In this way the body types contribute a great deal to whatever understanding of people I may be able to muster.

★   ★   ★

This second edition addresses the chief criticism leveled against the original publication of *Body Types* by including over twenty illustrations showing the types. Rather than attempting to precisely illustrate the exact body shape of each type, we have provided you with portraits of the types as models, or exemplars, of the themes articulated within each type. Since the seven body types are both visually recognizable and infinitely varied, the only guarantee that we can identify types is to gain a familiarity with the quality of energy associated with each type. It is this quality that the portraits are intended to communicate.

I have also attempted, in the new Introduction, to address the many inquiries I have received over the last few years about the possible connections between body types and the system of nine *personality* types associated with the enneagram. I hope this material will clarify these connections to some degree, and prove useful to students of both systems.

Also new are the pages between each principal type that deal with the circulation of types on the enneagram, and those which portray the *transitional* types—the half-steps on the enneagram. These additions accord with the greater emphasis this edition gives to the circulation of energy on the enneagram, and less on the individual points. Summaries at the end of each chapter devoted to the principal types help to bring together the disparate material presented in each case. These summaries also include detailed physical descriptions of each type taken from the work of William Benham, who is treated in more depth in the Introduction.

★　★　★

It is obvious to me now that the system of the seven types of humanity is quite old, perhaps much older than I had ever imagined during twenty years of studying and living with the types. I hope that those who come in contact here with the types will be stimulated to their own researches, and that the study of the body types will gain an even better footing than it has had for many, many years.

Joel Friedlander
Yorktown, New York
September, 1992

PART I

The World
of Types

Introduction

To be able to see that people are types is a remarkable, even shattering, experience. People are quite right to think it strange that something this obvious should have escaped them, but it has. It's as strange as never having noticed the color of your own hair, how tall your wife is, or something equally foolish.

Yet we all have a feel for types; we know the kind of people we're attracted to, for instance, and the ones that always rub us the wrong way. It just never occurred to us to look deeper into these feelings or to see whether there was more meaning in them. And it never dawned on us that there might be an entire *system* of these types that could help to organize what we already know about people in an entirely new way.

It's difficult to admit that we could know types if we were told about them. We won't believe it. If we're presented with a systematic explanation for our sense of types and shown what types look like and how to find them, we're skeptical. Even if it's explained to us that we could see other people's body types, and by doing so revolutionize our understanding, the whole idea seems unbelievable, it seems repugnant, or it seems simply impossible.

Of course, the notion that people are types—that they can be classified according to some fixed set of traits—is hardly a new idea, it's one of the most ancient. It's an idea that punctuates the early history of science, finds a place in the teachings of many primitive religions and has been forgotten, overlooked or debunked more times, in more places, by more people than we can count.

Thinking of people as specific types, and using those types to organize and illuminate our understanding of one another, has never really died out. It still has a hold on our imagination and continues to be fashionable today. Looking at some of the ways in which the idea of types has occurred before, how it was formulated and how it was practiced, may demonstrate that the idea of types isn't so strange after all—most of us have just stopped taking it as seriously as people once did.

Astrology

The first of these ways of classifying people—and by far the most familiar—is astrology. Who hasn't been fascinated by the possibilities that seem hidden in one's own astrological type—one's sign—and in the information that's supposed to come along with it? Who hasn't wondered whether there are truly insights to be gained from astrology's systematic definition of people?

I know I have. And almost everybody I meet must have some interest as well, because it's hard to come across anyone who doesn't know their sign and a little bit about what it's supposed to say about them. We've all been introduced to the fellow who opens his conversation with an astrological aside, "I'm a Capricorn." He's pleased his new boss is a

Gemini because he's always gotten along with Geminis in the past.

These common situations acknowledge, however unconsciously, the existence of types. While we may not delve any further into astrology than an occasional glance at the newspaper, neither do we forget our sign, nor completely lose the vestiges of our identification with it.

Ancient Gods

We can look to the ancient gods of Greece for another example of the historical existence of types. The Greeks of antiquity saw their gods not just as deities, but as representatives of their own inner drives—those universal forces that move us all, like passion, anger, love, patriotism or jealousy. The influence of the gods was exactly the influence of one or another of these drives, and the struggles amongst the gods, told and retold in legend and song, were also reflections of man's inner conflicts.

Apollo and Dionysus make a good example. Apollo exemplified order and reason; he was at odds with Dionysus, the proponent of sensuality and license. But each of us is split along these lines, our own cool reason contending with our impulse to let go, to indulge all our appetites to their maximum.

What the Greeks valued most of all was the harmony that could be achieved through a balance of these forces, the harmony created when both logic and license play their part, and in which neither completely dominates. When Apollo reigns it is reason that rules our actions; Dionysus makes us long for relaxation and release, for forgetting the duties that confine us. A man who is chiefly swayed by one or the other, who always follows either reason or release, could be assigned the attributes of that god. Apollo or Dionysus would rule him, and determine what type of man he is. And just as the mythological Apollo and Dionysus will never resolve their differences, so we must find the way within ourselves to bring these forces into harmony.

The Planetary World and the Days of the Week

Seven of these gods became associated with the seven heavenly bodies visible from the Earth with the naked eye, and their qualities have been bound together ever since. These connections have lasted through more than two thousand years and occupy a place now in the names we use for the planets and the days of the week. Each day has its god, and we have no difficulty in considering the whole week as a complete and self-contained system.

Monday belongs to the moon, ruled by Selene; Tuesday is Mars' day, under Ares; Mercury presides over Wednesday, the day of Hermes; Thursday belongs to Jupiter, whose god is Zeus; Friday is Venus' day, ruled by Aphrodite; Saturday is Saturn-day, the old Greek Kronos; and Sunday is the day of the Sun, ruled not by Apollo, but by Phoebus. Although we use these names every day we've forgotten their ancient origins. Like so much of our ancient heritage, the beliefs that built this system have lost their power, and no longer move us in the same way.

Cathedral Builders

About twelve hundred years closer to home—during the Gothic era—the idea of types appears again as one element in the symbolism invented by the builders of the great cathedrals. I'm referring particularly to twenty-eight figures that once ranged across the face of the Cathedral of Notre Dame in Paris, presumably sculptures of ancient kings.

But there's also a tradition that claims these figures represented body types, were meant to demonstrate a knowledge of types and were intended to instruct an illiterate populace in this knowledge through visible examples. The twenty-eight are the result of seven basic types multiplied by the four kinds of dispositions each type might have.

Some of these statues, 'lost' during the destruction that accompanied the French Revolution, have recently been unearthed and put on display. I saw them in New York, when they were exhibited briefly some years ago, and also at the Cluny Museum in Paris, their permanent home. I was unable to tell whether they are, in fact, meant to represent types, but several of these grave, intent faces emanate a force that's in all really transcendental art; they hint at universal laws.

Alchemy

The idea of types surfaced again in the Middle Ages, when it was championed by the alchemists—the mystic chemists of that time. Besides pioneering the systematic study of chemistry, they also devised a scheme of human types. It was built, as so many others have been, on the planetary model.

The alchemists wanted to fix the actions and interactions of metals that were important to their experiments in transmutation; they thought each of these metals was ruled by one of the seven visible planets. But these alchemists also used the same information to classify people. They decided that each man had a preponderance of one of the basic metals, and that this preponderance determined, among other things, a man's temperament, his physique and his susceptibility to specific illnesses.

It's melancholy to consider the medieval alchemists today. Their experiments, based on unprovable theories, couldn't withstand the pressure of constant failure. The alchemists proved incapable of actually conjuring up the gold their theories predicted they would. Yet it was an enlightened philosophy that led them to pursue their strange science, a philosophy intimately bound up with mysticism and the quest for human perfection.

The alchemists with the most profound aspirations weren't simply trying to amass personal wealth. They were trying to prove that the laws that ruled their philosophy could be applied to every level of existence, the material world as well as the spiritual—that they were objective laws.

Literature

There's no lack of types in literature, where we expect to find them. After all, much of the pleasure and a good deal of the insight we get from literature come from our ability to see a character struggling within the confines of his typical behavior. We appreciate these symbolic characters especially when they remind us of people we know—they come to represent that particular type in our thinking. Literary characters often become archetypes for whole classes of people and enable us to objectify, and to explain, their behavior.

Shakespeare's *Othello* rings with this use of character, although body types only provide the stage on which he built this remarkable play. Othello, the Moor, is courageous, impetuous and passionate; he's a picture of *Mars,* on whose behalf he wages the wars of state. Iago operates by deceit, treachery and calculation, lying easily whenever it's necessary to further his diabolical ends; he's a caricature of all the worst sides of *Mercury*. The action of the play as it descends to its inevitable and murderous conclusion springs largely from the instinctive antagonism of these two types.

Characters like Othello and Iago, locked together in their tragic destiny for all time, never change. As individuals they're incapable of change precisely because they're unable to alter a course once they've embarked on it. I've watched them play out this dance of death over and over, as others have for hundreds of years, and it never fails to move me. Shakespeare has stretched the impulses in their types almost to the point of caricature. They've passed beyond simple examples of their types and gone on to become bloody exaggerations of their most murderous features. In every performance their involuntary behavior fires the unreasoned hatred in their types, and defeats them.

Modern Psychology

The advent of 'scientific psychology' has seen the idea of body types decline in importance; it's treated as 'unscientific.' One of the few exceptions to this trend was the American anthropologist, William Sheldon. Having photographed thousands of subjects, Sheldon arrived at a method of dividing people into three types. He attempted to link three distinct kinds of temperaments to the three types of bodies in his scheme. These divisions were based on his theory that each type had developed from a different layer of cells in the embryo, and he named them after these three cellular levels; ectomorph, mesomorph and endomorph.

Sheldon's ectomorph grows from the ectoderm, the outer layer of cells in the embryo, from which also grow the skin, hair, nails and the nervous system. These ectomorphs are wiry and have a surplus of nervous energy. His mesomorph grows from the middle layer of cells, which also gives rise to the skeletal, muscular and connective tissue as well as the circulatory, excretory and reproductive systems. Mesomorphs have a muscular, sturdy build. Endomorphs are reputed to grow from the innermost cell layer, from which the digestive glands, the lining of the alimentary tract and the lungs also grow. Endomorphs are the heavyweights among us.

This scheme, which received widespread publicity, remains popular today. Carol Saltus, a modern practitioner who has refined Sheldon's ideas and attempted to make them into a practical study, has said that, "Sheldon's achievement has provided us with a powerful new tool for self-knowledge, an indispensable key to unlocking the secrets of the self." She has also presented systematic psychological profiles of Sheldon's three types.

The attraction of this system has a good deal to do with its simplicity. And while it has provided the impetus for some further research into the idea that psychological traits might correspond to the form of the physical body, it has mostly

ENDOMORPH	MESOMORPH	ECTOMORPH
Sociable	Independent	Private
Relaxed	Assertive	Tense
Comfort-loving	Physically active	Mentally active
Optimistic	Adventurous	Apprehensive
Generous	Ambitions	Excitable
Practical	Insensitive	Sensitive
Stable	Combative	Passionate
Calm	Bold	Quick

Sheldon's Types
(from Saltus)

lingered on the fringes of respectability. However, researchers in another discipline have attacked the same problem, and we can look to the fruits of their investigations for information that throws an entirely different light on the theory of types.

Endocrinology

Endocrinology, which studies the glands that regulate many of the body's systems through hormones, has produced a different method for typing people. Dr. Louis Berman was one of the chief proponents of this idea, and he assembled an entire plan of types built on glandular imbalances.

Berman thought that the over-activity of each gland produced a type that bore all the markings of that gland's functions. He looked back through history for examples and included in his books illustrations for each of these types. His descriptions included not only the appearance of the types but the results of their particular glandular imbalance on their personality. For instance, his adrenal type usually had bright red hair, freckles and an explosive disposition. Although the nature of each type cannot be perfectly aligned with the activity of its corresponding endocrine gland, the intimate connection between these two systems is full of promise. An outline of these connections, "Glands and Behavior," is provided in Part III.

Unfortunately, Dr. Berman's theories have been neglected even more than Sheldon's have, and are almost unknown today. Perhaps it's been the rise of democratic thinking, with its insistence that 'all men are created equal,' that's closed the door on the study of human types. It goes against the grain of our education. We can't imagine a typology that isn't bigotry, or worse. Now the idea of physical types is in ill-repute, scorned as quackery or feared as prejudice, and these attitudes can shut us off from any real study of body types.

Esoteric Schools

Several of the systems of classifying people that I've mentioned grew from common roots, even though they flowered in different ways. They were schemes originally conceived, interpreted and transmitted by unusual teachers in unusual schools, all of whom were connected in one way or another with the practice of mysticism. Among the astrologers and astronomers, the builders of the gothic cathedrals and the alchemists were some who focused all their energy on inner transformation, searching for the knowledge that would lead them to a personal, mystical revelation. The idea of body types would have occupied a significant place in their interest.

However, the little knowledge that remains from these schools describes the types in arcane, symbolic or forgotten languages; it doesn't tell us how to observe them ourselves. It's possible that the methods invented for applying the knowledge of types were kept on the hidden, esoteric side of these teachings. They may never have carried farther than the sound of a teacher's voice. Since these methods would invariably have been designed for the people of a specific time in a specific culture, they wouldn't have lived nearly as long as the philosophy that produced them. In any event, someone looking for a way to make use of this knowledge would have found, until recently, very little to help him.

William Benham's Seven Types

Oddly enough, the only specific record we have of the plan of the seven types is from an extremely unlikely source; William Benham, one of the nineteenth century originators of modern palmistry. And this source is, in some ways, as mysterious as the lost alchemists and astronomers of old.

Benham implied that he learned of the system of types at the age of thirteen from gypsies. He then went on to dedicate his life to the study of character as revealed in people's palms, and "read" the hands of many of the most eminent people of his day. Although he does not indicate how he derived his understanding of types from a study of palms, he succeeded in re-creating on his own the entire system of seven types, and learned to identify their body shapes as well as their palms.

In fact, Benham's descriptions of the seven types leaves no doubt whatsoever that the typology he is dealing with is identical to the one you will read about as you explore the body types in later chapters. This remarkable coincidence can be interpreted in various ways. From one point of view, it may be a rather clear indication that the information we have about the seven types is *objective;* that it is capable of discovery and verification by independent observers. Or we might see it as confirmation that knowledge of the types has always been maintained by "schools" of various kinds and only released at widely-spaced intervals. However, we might also come to the conclusion that the various sources for the information on the types actually knew of each other's work but, for some reason unknown to us, never indicated this knowledge. Perhaps we will never know which of these scenarios is correct.

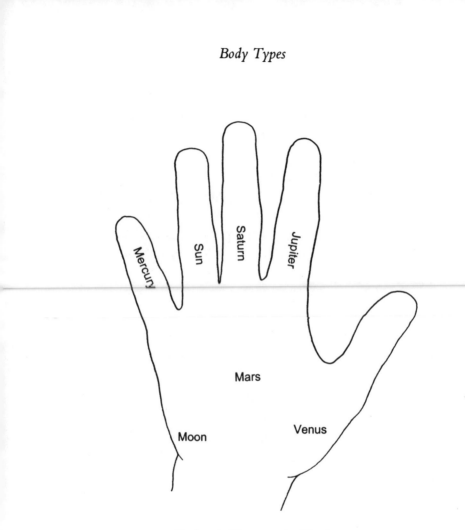

Benham's Types on the Hand

Because Benham's descriptions of the physical nature of each type are so detailed, they have been edited and appended to the summaries that appear at the end of each chapter to add information that will help in identifying the types. In his major work, *The Laws of Scientific Hand Reading,* published in 1900, he says, "These types look alike, and I shall give you mental illustrations of their appearance. Thus, knowing each type well, what they look like, how they reason, live, think, work, play, treat their fellows, or marry, as well as their natural occupations and peculiarities, you can, when you meet one of a certain type, dissect him with ease, knowing him better than he knows himself."

Since Benham was primarily—if not exclusively—a student of human nature as revealed in the hand, it is instructive to see how he placed the seven types on the topography of the hand. Benham says that the index finger belongs to Jupiter, the middle finger to Saturn, the ring finger to Solar and the pinkie to Mercury. Venus is located on the mound at the base of the thumb, Mars across the palm, and Lunar on the pad of the palm opposite the thumb. In response to the question of why these specific regions denote the various types, Benham says, "To this question the answer must be given that at this time we have not fully solved the mystery," but goes on to describe why the hand itself may reveal the activity of the mind. In addition, he quotes what he calls the oldest treatise on palmistry—by Aristotle—to show its long provenance. Here is a part of Aristotle's presentation of the seven primal types associated with the hand, in which we see the importance given to the actual influence of the planets:

> The Thumb we to Dame *Venus* Rules commit;
> *Jove* the fore Finger rules as he thinks fit;
> Old *Saturn* does the middle Finger guide,
> And o'er the Ring Finger *Sol* does still preside;
> The outside Brawn pale *Cynthia* does direct,
> And into the Hallow *Mars* does most inspect:
> The little Finger does to *Merc'ry* fall,
> Which is the nimblest Planet of them all.

Benham had no doubt that the scheme of types was of ancient origin, although he gives little indication of his sources for this statement. He said, "The ancient theory of the seven distinct types of people begins with the idea that the human race was undoubtedly constructed by its Creator under a definite plan. There was no hit-or-miss in shaping and putting together the inhabitants of this globe." In this sense, Benham's ideas on type agree with our own, and imply that the integrated whole of the system of body types is a great deal older than we may have originally thought. It will be some time, and require further research into its history for us to be able to show with any certainty the earliest origins of this remarkable system.

The Reappearance of Types

I suppose it was natural, if not inevitable, that when the idea of body types appeared again it would be as part of a system of thought linked to practical mysticism. This time, it surfaced within the stream of events that carried an Armenian-Greek from southern Russia off to Asia in search of hidden knowledge. It was a stream that eventually swept him, along with his circle of students, completely out of Russia during the revolution of 1917 and washed him onto Europe's shore. By the time he came to the notice of the West this linguist, philosopher, traveller, dance instructor, musician and mystic had evolved a remarkable and comprehensive system for the study and improvement of men, and had become one of the world's chief channels for esoteric doctrine. His name was George Gurdjieff.

Gurdjieff's Influence

One of the doctrines Gurdjieff incorporated into his teaching came from the wealth of mystical writings ascribed to the ancient Egyptian, Hermes Trismegistus. This is the same Hermes, of course, who figured so prominently in the thoughts of medieval alchemists sweating over the peculiar devices that were the ritual tools of their arcane art. This parallel isn't so strange when you compare the authentic teachings of alchemy and their stress on inner transformation with the ideas that Gurdjieff taught; they seem to have had many of the same goals in mind.

This particular doctrine describes the world as harmonious, objective and unified. In this world everything is related to everything else by virtue of laws that apply equally to all scales of existence. The doctrine was expressed in a formula: *As above, so below.*

Gurdjieff used this formula for the same reasons the alchemists did, perhaps even from the same point of view. He taught that every iota of reality was ruled by identical laws, and that a knowledge of how these laws affect a process on one level could also be used to understand similar processes on other levels. He called the laws that contained such universal power *objective laws,* and a good deal of his method depended on his students understanding and eventually embodying these laws.

When it came to the study of man, Gurdjieff's philosophy showed these laws in action. He taught that as long as a man remains ignorant of these laws he will never find a way to manipulate them to his own advantage. Although Gurdjieff left almost no detailed knowledge of types behind him, he knew and studied the idea himself. Man's subjugation to the rigid, mechanical and unyielding laws that he did describe is deeply embedded throughout the body of his thought.

Peter Ouspensky was one of Gurdjieff's chief pupils, and a member of the group that had followed him out of Russia. Later he recounted, in *In Search of the Miraculous,* his time with Gurdjieff. In this book Ouspensky drew the broad outline of the methods he had been shown by which men could learn to observe these laws themselves, and by which they could change.

Both Gurdjieff and Ouspensky saw the study of human psychology as an individual exploration into human evolution; the aim of their teaching was the creation of "higher" men. Like the alchemists, they reached far back into the history of practical mysticism for their materials, and there found what they required: concepts that would breathe life into their idea of human evolution. They constructed models of man based on these ancient teachings and used these models to put the tools of self-study, self-change and self-realization into the hands of their students.

Rodney Collin

Although body types didn't receive much attention from Gurdjieff or Ouspensky, it was one of Ouspensky's students, Rodney Collin, who finally gathered the loose strands into a coherent whole. Collin, an Englishman who moved to Mexico after Ouspensky's death in 1947, connected the old knowledge to new, and in his *Theory of Celestial Influence* laid the groundwork for the scheme of types.

One of the chief contributions Collin made in his description of types was to assemble a mass of apparently unrelated knowledge in one place. Using the work of Dr. Berman, he connected the insights of modern endocrinology to the lore of archaic priests and shamans. He hadn't set out specifically to explain body types; he was involved in an attempt to explain everything, and to unearth all the connections he could between modern science and the philosophy he'd inherited from Ouspensky.

Four Levels of the System

In the *Theory of Celestial Influence* Collin introduced the analogy that lies behind the theory of body types. In its present form this analogy compares four different levels: the action and the interaction of the endocrine glands; the characteristics of the archaic planets; the traits of the classic Western gods; and the work and relationships of men. The shape of this analogy was formed by the parallels Collin found among its parts. Its force was supplied by the similarities in its disparate worlds of glands, planets, gods and men.

It was the addition of the endocrine glands to the mix that set Collin's idea of types apart from earlier versions and

Spiral of glands with their corresponding planets, from Collin. He said the relation between the two could be mathematically plotted.

revitalized this ancient study. In many ways the connection between glands and behavior remains tantalizing, but out of reach. It promises new ways to comprehend men but it remains clouded and inscrutable. But studying the glands helps us to understand types because the world of the endocrine glands parallels the other worlds of the body type theory, and like them contains a variety of individuals organized into a complete, cohesive and universal system that can be applied to anyone.

Each Level is Wholistic

We all have the same endocrine glands, and the glands always contribute the same functions to the work of the body. The planets, moons and other members of the solar system hang in their fixed relations in space. Society continues to make use of the work of different kinds of people. And each of us has within us all the primal urges that the old gods represent. Each member of each system—gland, planet, god or man—always supplies the same kind of work within its community.

For an example spanning these various worlds, look at Mars, which is related to the adrenal glands. Humans can't live without their adrenals; the adrenals have too many unique and urgent jobs to do. The rush of adrenaline is a natural and necessary human function. The war god Mars guards the borders, repels intruders, destroys the weak—that is, he stands for the guarding, repelling, destroying that are natural and necessary in every society. The planet that bears his name is the 'red' planet, the 'angry' planet. And it's the pugnacious Martial body type that contributes the warriors, the pioneers and the fighters to humanity.

This theory reduces the types to seven different kinds; a number so small it threatens to squash any chance we had to be unique. But each of us is a different combination of the same, familiar features; our precise tuning and peculiar rhythms are what distinguish us as individuals. Blending the few basic types still creates the incredible diversity we see in people wherever we look. And while it might seem that studying types would crush our sense of our own uniqueness, Rodney Collin, Peter Ouspensky, George Gurdjieff and their ancestors were actually working to promote a less mechanical, more spiritual, individuality.

The Enneagram's Nine Personality Types

Another more recent development in the *Fourth Way,* as Gurdjieff's system has come to be called, that relates to the study of body types is the introduction of the nine personality types. This study is said to have been introduced to the West by the Chilean spiritual teacher Oscar Ichazo. It is now written about and taught by a growing number of practitioners, including Helen Palmer, Margaret Frings Keyes, Richard Rohr, Don Richard Riso and Claudio Naranjo. In this book I have principally used Helen Palmer's presentation for the basis of my remarks.

This system also uses the *enneagram,* (a nine-pointed figure explained in more detail in the next chapter) to explain a complete set of behavioral types. In this enneagram system the types are named for the numbers of the points on which they occur. However, various writers have also created their own names for the types, not all of which agree. These types are not physical types so much as they are developmental, or behavioral types. They show how particular models of development can lead to specific forms of fixation and dependency. Palmer has pointed out that this system can usefully be treated as a study of *chief feature,* a Gurdjieffian idea that attempts to locate, for each individual, the one attitude we hold about ourselves that represents a fundamental error of self-perception, and around which we mistakenly form the rest of our picture of ourselves.

Essence and Personality

Since the nine-type system uses the enneagram, as does the system of body types itself, the question has naturally arisen among students of both systems as to how, or if, the two systems are related. It seems to me now that there is a relationship of a kind between these two powerful ways of self-discovery. An understanding of this connection, however, can only be achieved if we first understand Gurdjieff's ideas of *essence* and *personality.*

There are many detailed maps of human psychology in the system that Gurdjieff had taught, and one of the most interesting comparisons he drew was between what we are born with, and what we acquire as we mature. He called the inborn being, naturally enough, our *essence.* This essence is seen as incorporating both the accumulated genetic history represented by our heredity, as well as the more mysterious elements that come to us from quite outside our hereditary endowment, such as our inborn tendencies, basic interests and aptitudes. *Personality,* on the other hand, is everything that we have acquired of a more superficial nature since our birth, and which becomes the instrument through which we interact with the world.

Neither essence nor personality is a static thing; both can grow, mature and change, but in radically different ways, and with different effects. Essence is affected by ideas, events and impressions that reach us directly, that touch our core. It matures as a result of accumulated experience, and changes that take place in essence are more or less permanent. Many things about essence cannot be changed at all, in fact, in the same way that we cannot change the kind of hair we have, how tall we are, or our fundamental type of body structure.

Personality begins to form later, as the child meets with expectations in its environment, and begins to modify its behavior to accord with—or struggle against—those expectations. Personality eventually becomes the "organ" or "filter" through which the essential person knows the world,

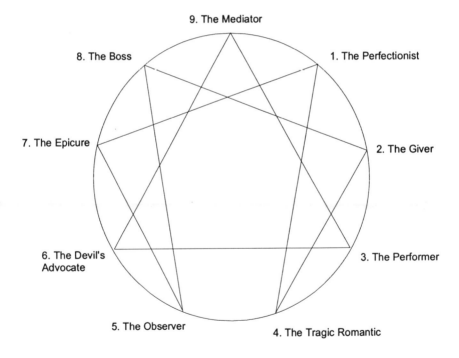

The Nine Personality Types
(from Palmer)

and the container for all one's specific knowledge of things. In this role, it grows to protect the otherwise unprotected essence that is far too sensitive and, in some ways, too primitive, to survive a day-to-day existence. All our intellectual achievements, all our learned behaviors, all our acquired emotions are parts of our personality.

To get a simplistic idea of the difference between these two, and perhaps an inkling of the kinds of difficulties one can encounter through this new idea, let's go back to hair. Although there is no way to change the *kind* of hair we have—essence—there are thousands of ways to make it *look* different—personality. I can flatten it, curl it, perm it, color it, cover it, or have it pulled out. In each case, it is my personality trying to influence what I really am—my essence.

The Two "Enneagram" Systems

In the same way we can see these two, apparently inconsistent systems of typology, as two ways of slicing the same pie. Body types, as discussed in this book, are *essence* types. They are inborn and unchangeable. If you are a Saturnine type, nothing you can do will make you into a Jovial. It doesn't matter in the least what kind of upbringing you've had, where you were raised, whether you are a sinner or a saint: you will remain a Saturn.

The nine-point enneagram types, however, are *personality* types. They reflect early conditioning and say much more about the details of our psychological makeup. They show us where we have false perceptions about ourselves, how we can remove limiting behaviors, and why we might have developed in the ways we have.

This distinction gives us the most useful picture of these two systems. It shows that each system can be useful to us for learning to think about ourselves differently, and for exploring our psychology in revealing new ways. To extend our example, it is now possible to see that an essence Saturn could well be any of the nine personality types. To use Palmer's names for the types, our Saturn could be a *Mediator* (the type at point nine on the enneagram), a *Perfectionist* (point one), a *Performer* (point three), or any of the other types.

In fact, it does seem that certain personality types occur with more frequency amongst specific body types, but there has been no research into this nascent study other than gathering evidence that is purely anecdotal. Perhaps this will be an area of examination in the future. However, we can safely say that the combination of both studies is far more potent for the student who takes the time to learn them, than the study of one system is on its own. And because these systems have a common origin in the work of Gurdjieff, there is no real reason for one to exclude the other.

Robert Burton

Rodney Collin had tried to indicate, in a general way, how to observe body types. This turned out to be crucial to the eventual development of body types, because the method that Collin, Gurdjieff and Ouspensky taught was based on direct experience and personal observation. In this *Fourth Way* system, if you can't verify the ideas yourself, they're useless. Body types, to be taken seriously, had to be capable of being experienced directly if it was going to find any further expression in this line of development.

In 1970 another Fourth Way teacher, Robert Burton, began to teach this system of types to a small group of students. Starting from the very brief descriptions that Collin had left, and incorporating Dr. Berman's work, Burton began to piece together the system of types once again.

During the initial period of this new exploration into body types a great deal of information began to come from the direct observations of Burton and his students. They found that every type was clearly visible and, as Benham had said, "There are well-defined specimens of all these types on the streets of our cities to-day, and they can be easily recognized." Over the years, the basic information that had been the basis of this study began to be elaborated by discovering the seven types in the people around them. Burton and his students became so adept at this study that by 1973 they were able to privately publish the first major treatment of body types that had been attempted in the twentieth century. Burton told his students that the study of types had become his specialty, his unique contribution to the accumulation of Fourth Way lore. The thousands of students of Burton's teaching, both past and present, probably represent the largest group of people currently studying this system of types.

However, looking at the remarkable history of body types throughout our cultural history, we must assume that this is only the most recent, and probably not the last, expression of the oldest and most useful way we have yet discovered of categorizing people's essential nature. And to my way of thinking, no more potent tool has yet been devised that is as capable of revealing the shape of our essential nature, and of making it readily observable and open to our personal study. It is this power that has made the study of the seven ancient body types live once again.

Body Type Basics

I've found that types are easy to see, that anyone can learn to grasp them if they search a little. Like all searches, this one begins best with the right tools, with a general idea of where we are going, and with some pointers left for us along the way by the people who have gone before. First, it's important to get a grip on some of the ideas that are basic to all of the types.

The Enneagram

One of the primary tools we use when studying body types is a diagram that George Gurdjieff introduced as part of his philosophy. It consists of three separate figures merged into one, and is known as the *enneagram* because it has nine principle points. (The prefix *ennea* stands for the number nine.)

The outside figure is a circle around which are nine equally spaced points. Each point is numbered. The topmost point is nine, the one to its right one, the next two, and so on clockwise around the circle. The second figure is the equal-sided triangle created by linking the points nine, six and three. The third figure connects the remaining six points in the order; one, four, two, eight, five, seven. This yields a rising, crossing shape of six lines, independent of both outer circle and inner triangle. While Gurdjieff used this enneagram to illustrate many of his ideas about man and much of his cosmology, we principally use the inner, six-pointed figure of the enneagram when studying body types.

Each type occupies one of these points except Solar, which has no precise location. Lunar starts the progression at point one and, proceeding in the same order we used to generate this figure, we come to Venus at four, Mercury at two, Saturn at eight, Mars at five and Jupiter at seven, from which point the figure completes itself by returning to one.

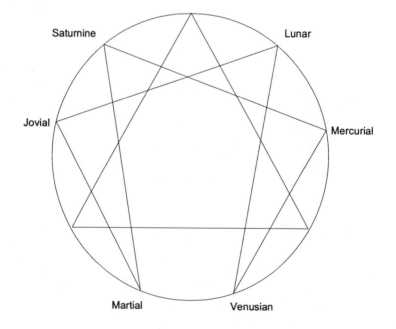

The Enneagram of Body Types

No 'Pure' Types

Within this scheme, completely pure, unmixed types simply don't exist. Each of us is situated at some point on this line of progression and the unique blend of our type contains the influences of every type.

It's when we consider the types as archetypes, as symbols of our primitive passions, that we have to look at them separately. Then they epitomize those passions and the desires and perceptions potential in each of us. Isolated, the types become the separate but equal members of a pantheon, a set of glands, a planetary system or a society of men. But the people we meet are amalgams in whom one type has been alloyed with a neighbor, and who show traces of them all.

Circulation of Types

The flow of the types through the points around the enneagram occupies one of the chief places in the idea of body types. The direction of this flow determines the order in which the types occur, and its structure implies many of their characteristics. When we consider this flow through the points of the enneagram, we see that the body types are actually a continuous development of energy through a series of distinct human expressions. This perspective shows us that the scheme of types is a wholistic expression of the variety of human form, rather than a set of six or seven categories into which each person must fit.

For a practical understanding of this flow, we can say that everyone seems to fall somewhere on this line of circulation. The direction is always the same, and we speak about types as developments within this order: Lunar, Lunar-Venusian, Venusian, Venusian-Mercury, and so on. In this way we arrive at thirteen body types as a complete manifestation of the theory of types: the six types whose traits cluster around the principal, defining points of the enneagram; six *transitional types* that represent the half-steps or mixture of any two adjacent types between the principal points; and the Solar type, sitting somewhere outside the general circulation. These thirteen types then would give us a more or less complete set from which we can approach our practical study. In fact, we will find that most people we observe are mixtures of one kind or another.

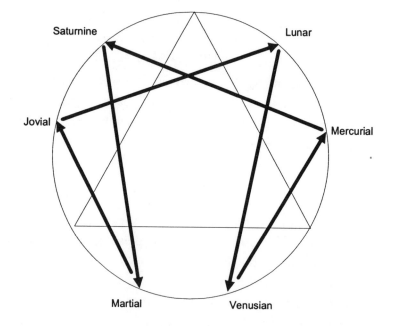

The Circulation of Types on the Enneagram

An Example

Let me show you what I mean by using myself as the example closest to hand. Since my body type is ruled by Jupiter and the Moon, I am a *Jovial-Lunar* type. (Not a Lunar-Jovial, because we must follow the order of the circulation.) I can find occasional traits of Venus, or Saturn or the others in my attitudes and behavior, but mostly what I see in myself arises about equally from Jovial and Lunar. Even more, although my type shares essential traits with both Jovial and Lunar, the Jovial-Lunar is a distinct type itself, and creates its own blend of behavior as do all the other steps on the enneagram.

Positive and Negative Types

The structure that's described by the rhythmic, repetitive flow of the enneagram helps to understand two of the basic traits of body types. These traits play an overriding part in determining the outline of our body and our general appearance. They regulate our thinking, skew our relationships and color our most fundamental attitudes.

First, each type is either positive or negative, in the way that an electrical charge is positive or negative. This charge alternates throughout the flow of types starting at Lunar, a negative type. Venusian is positive, Mercury negative, Saturn positive, Mars negative and Jovial positive. Solar, which doesn't participate in the circulation of types, is positive as well. Whether positive or negative, this trait slants our view of life and prejudices many parts of our behavior.

Simply put, positive types are more optimistic. They disregard the difficult and unpleasant sides of life, and seem to possess a generally constructive mentality. Negative types are more skeptical, restless and dissatisfied. They take a dimmer, more careful view of life, and frequently can't avoid noticing its faults, its flaws and its frequent failures.

Active and Passive Types

The second basic characteristic of the types is how active or passive they are. Here the enneagram is divided differently; the active types are Mercury, Saturn and Mars, the passive ones are Jovial, Lunar and Venusian. But these attributes don't alternate like the positive and negative ones did. Activity and passivity, which correspond to masculine and feminine principles, wax and wane as they progress through the types, and subtly color each type's vitality and tone.

In this progression we find the energy and orientation of types at its most passive in Lunar. It continues to be passive through Venusian, enters the active sphere at Mercury, peaks in Saturn and declines through Mars. Finally, it passes back across the threshold of passivity at Jovial and the cycle is complete. Solar, outside this circulation, is an active type. Because the active force isn't static, but evolves through distinct stages under a variety of influences before it turns passive, each type represents a specific quality or mixture of these influences.

Mercury, for instance, still has traces of the feminine energy associated with Venus, the type before it, while Jovial has traces of the masculine energy of its predecessor, Mars. Venusians, whose minds and bodies are by far the quietest of all the types, also seem to be sunk deepest in passivity. But it's actually Lunar, with the passive energy of Jovial behind, and the passive energy of Venusian in front, that is the purest expression of the passive, feminine principle.

Again, although Mars accumulates the active energy and is the most violently active type, and although Mercury carries activity that's young and rising from Venus, it is Saturn, despite its slow and introspective bearing, that occupies the principle role of activity, and that overflows with the tide of masculinity as it travels between Mercury and Mars.

Combining Basic Traits

A simple way to understand and learn to identify the active and passive qualities of people is to look at the ways they use their time. A quiet Sunday afternoon finds one person cleaning his house or tinkering with his car. Someone else is satisfied to curl up with a good book and not go out all day. Those who must have something to do are usually active types.

The combination of active, passive, positive and negative traits yields four combinations for the seven types. Lunar is the only body type that's both passive and negative, while Saturn is its opposite, active and positive. Venusian and Jovial are passive, positive types, and are balanced by Mercury and Mars, both active and negative.

Active and positive people—Saturns and Solars—are full of plans, building houses, founding organizations, working on their careers or recruiting friends to help with their many

	ACTIVE	PASSIVE
POSITIVE	Saturn Solar	Venusian Jovial
NEGATIVE	Mercury Mars	Lunar

Body Type Combinations

Body Types

Lunar

Lunar-Venusian

Mercury

Mercury-Saturn

Mars

Mars-Jovial

Solar

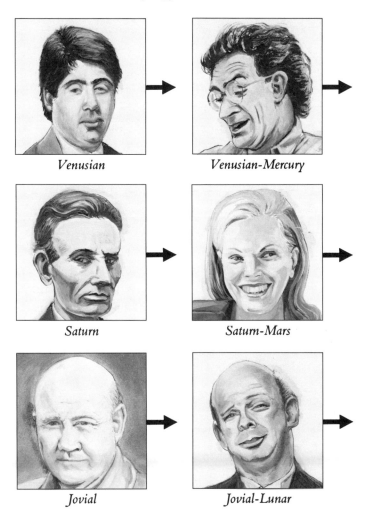

Venusian	*Venusian-Mercury*
Saturn	*Saturn-Mars*
Jovial	*Jovial-Lunar*

Circulation of types: Details from the portraits of the types are shown here in their circulation to indicate the progression of "energy" as it moves through the types. Traditionally, Lunar stands at the beginning. You can see subtle transitions from one type to another, passing through the twelve principal and transitional types. From Jovial-Lunar the circulation returns to Lunar to begin its endless variations once again. Solar is shown at the left, outside this circulation.

projects. Martials and Mercuries, active types who are also negative, are restless and don't need a reason to move; they're compelled. But wherever they go, trouble follows. They can't watch a movie without noticing the jumpy editing, they can't eat at a new restaurant without criticizing the service. They're glad to point out these defects to anyone who'll listen and may pick a fight with you if you don't agree.

Venusians and Jovials, who are both passive and positive, are playful and popular. They're warm and generous, even benevolent. They're always there to help friends or strangers in a fix, whether it's a bowl of chicken soup that's needed, or ready cash. They can be sensuous and fun, but are often disorganized and lazy. Lunars, the only passive and negative type, are loners. They're unhappy with the way things are, but only contribute complaints. They think the weather's awful, their job's a bore and life hardly worth living. As if being passive isn't enough, they may lack either the desire to change anything, or the energy, or both.

The Flow Contains the Remedy

The flow of the enneagram, however, also contains the remedy each type needs in order to overcome its particular imbalance. By looking toward the type ahead, and at the strengths inherent in that type, each will find exactly what it needs to offset its own weaknesses.

For example, the Lunar who can't help keeping cool and distant, even in the storms of his own passion, will find in the warmth and openness of Venus an antidote, should he be able to acquire it, for his personal anguish, because he will learn to express himself to others. The dynamics involved in this circulation of the types around the enneagram, and the psychological insight and personal balance that it promises, are major contributions of the study of body types. As we explore each type in the chapters ahead we will delve into the meaning this circulation holds for each type.

Body Shapes Among the Types

One area that needs to be reckoned with is the variety of body *shapes* to be found within each body *type*. We could draw on the work of William Sheldon to shed light on this area, and say that there are endomorphs, ectomorphs and mesomorphs within each category. However, the Fourth Way system that has served as the springboard for the modern elaboration of the body types provides us with an even more potent way of looking at these body shapes. Indeed, it may even bring Sheldon's categories into the system whole.

The Fourth Way idea I am referring to is that of *center of gravity*. Briefly, this means that each of us has a tendency to relate to the world predominantly on the basis of attitudes that come from one particular group of functions; the intellect, the emotions or the physical realm. Or, in Helen Palmer's terms; the head, heart or belly. Gurdjieff said that these primal centers of functioning can actually be seen as differing *intelligences* within us and, if we knew which function ruled us, would go a long way toward describing our motives and basic outlook on the world.

For instance, an intellectual type might look at the world as things to be described, labeled, categorized. The emotional type is seeking reasons to experience their own feelings. Physical types inhabit a world of objects and spaces in relation to each other. At a concert, we can visualize the intellectual person following the progress of the score, the emotional type swept away by the feelings produced by the music, and the physical person entranced by the movement in the music and the sensations it produces within them. When attention strays, the intellectual might be lost in thoughts and thoughts about thoughts, the emotional type may become absorbed in a past or anticipated encounter with someone who elicits their feelings—positive or negative—and the physical type will begin to squirm and think about the projects to be done and places to go.

Fits Sheldon's Types

In addition, each of the three types has a distinct body character that somewhat approximates Sheldon's divisions. The intellectual people have the attenuated look of ectomorphs. They are more finely drawn than the others, and their fingers and toes will often be slender and delicate. Emotional people have the plump, rounded look of the endomorph. They are fleshy, have difficulty with their weight and their faces flush easily. Physical types have the powerful, muscular body of the mesomorph. They are compact, dense and well-toned.

Characteristics assigned to the three Sheldon types fit this scheme as well. Ectomorphs are sometimes characterized as mentally active and excitable, indications of an intellectual type. Endomorphs are said to be sociable and comfort-loving, traits also found in emotional types. And mesomorphs share with physical types the tendencies toward being physically active and adventurous. So there really is evidence to make these divisions usable in the study of the seven types.

Adding this overlay to the basic body types, we can say that there are, for instance, intellectual Martials, emotional Martials and physical Martials. Each of these three is a variation on the Martial theme, and has its own distinct character. And each would modify the basic Martial orientation, sometimes substantially. As with any other genuine categorization of people, those who share a particular orientation will be able to empathize with the others in their sphere. Emotional Martials will have, on some level, an immediate recognition of the motivating forces at work in an emotional Jovial, for example.

Indeed, this center of gravity—or predominating function—is so important that a truly complete treatment of the seven body types would need to take this division into account. However, this complete treatment is beyond the scope of the current work, and remains to be elaborated more fully.

Types of Relationships

We can also plot on the enneagram a picture of the forces that draw one type to another, or that repel them in disgust. In doing so we won't be surprised to find that opposites attract, and that blends of opposites create blends of attraction.

Lying on opposite sides of the enneagram, the pairs of types that are drawn to each other have qualities that, when combined, strike an uneasy but fascinating attraction. Saturn, which is positive, active and paternal, attracts and is attracted by negative, passive and childish Lunar. Jovial's positive, passive flamboyance is the perfect complement to Mercury's negative, active wit. Mars finds in the receptive Venus a welcome for all his active, negative energy. Solar, a type that mixes with the other six, depends on that mixture to establish attractions which mostly correspond to those that already exist between the other types.

These three bonds created by the three pairs of types are examples of universal kinds of relationships. The Lunar-Saturn bond stands for the push and pull of our connection to our family; it's undemonstrative but strong. The combination of Mercury and Jovial symbolizes our more social associations, like the waxing and waning of our circle of friends; here the emphasis is on variety, spontaneity and wit. The tie that binds Mars to Venus vibrates with the intensity between lovers; it's where our most disturbing emotions are found.

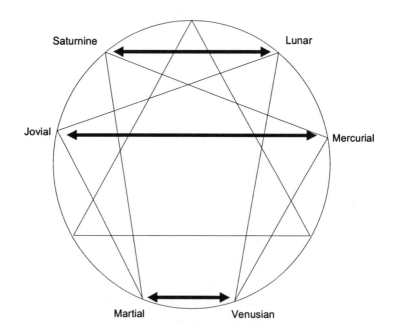

Attractions Across the Enneagram

Maybe each of us also has a type with which we just don't mix: the chemistry's all wrong. We repel each other with a natural force, and like the positive poles of two magnets we never get close enough to touch. Although we're aware enough of the other to exclude them, it's a hazy awareness, and undemanding. For us, these people just don't exist.

Mercury and Mars, however—the two active, negative types—repel each other more than any other combination on the enneagram. Their instinctive repulsion can be un-reasoned, immediate and violent. It is the opposition of forces that are too similar to mistake each other, and too different to endure each other. Their goals often look the same to everyone else but because they're approaching these goals from contrary directions, they risk the explosive impact of a head-on collision.

Each of these attractions and repulsions is a dynamic connection, fueled by the tension of opposites. Each contains not only the material to create powerful desires, but the seeds of equally powerful distaste. At the same time, these combinations can illustrate our inner world as well and describe the factions at war within us; then they tell us something about the nature of our own inner struggles.

What We See in Body Types

If we could spot the type of the friend sitting on our couch, our boss at the office, our lover, father or son, what exactly would we be seeing? Can we distinguish between characteristics that tell us their type and qualities that only individuals can possess? I think we can, but only if we remember that no matter how obvious a type seems to be, and no matter how abrupt our recognition of that type has been, there are no *typical* people.

Like any other method we might use to classify people, body types can be misunderstood, misrepresented or misused. Then the ideas produce fraud, bias or bigotry. These distortions aren't built into the idea of body types, but they happen anyway, because we confuse the types we see with the people in whom we're seeing them.

It's essential that we train ourselves to make this distinction. Without it we won't be able to learn about body types, or use our knowledge to deepen our understanding of people. The honesty of a friend, for instance, regularly and truly proved, is his alone, regardless of his type. Maybe he's a Martial, a type noted for frank comments and blunt evaluations. The hand of Mars will guide the form his honesty takes, and make it strike a frank and brutal note. Mars can't make him honest if he isn't, any more than Mercury can make someone dishonest, if he's committed to truth.

You can see this distinction in the action of a moment. If conditions demand honesty from our friend, it won't be Mars, but something deeper and more personal that will inspire him to be true to his conviction, to disregard his own chances, and tell you what he thinks.

If we notice nobility, deceit, intelligence, flexibility of mind, prejudice, courage, ambition or grace in the people we're observing, (or in ourselves, for that matter), we're seeing the signs of individuality—notes struck deep inside the framework that's provided by a body type.

I make a point of this distinction because in describing the types in the chapters ahead I have had to treat them whole. These aren't portraits of specific people. They're meant to suggest the themes that run through the types, the atmosphere that surrounds them, and the motives that drive them. The descriptions show the kinds of desires that we owe to our body types and the means by which we pursue those desires. Although they're abstractions, they're useful ones, and I invite you to use them to observe yourself and the people around you.

What We Receive from Body Types

People who study body types get a new angle on themselves almost immediately. They're jarred, and begin to see their own behavior in quite a different light. A person who starts to notice many signs of Jovial in himself, for instance, will also start to wonder why he's so proud of his generosity. Or he may look anew at the friends he so effortlessly collects, and realize that these friends may not know very much about him. He may begin to wonder, in fact, which of the qualities he's been so proud of are really his own.

While this Jovial has certainly had the edge taken off his pride, he's gained something as well. He no longer criticizes himself for rarely finishing projects, or for reading ten books at once; he knows that Jovials have a *periodic* nature—they never do one thing for long. He finds an explanation, although not a justification, for his wanton use of money. Although he's given up his pride in his typical, automatic acts, he's also dropped the burden of his equally automatic guilt.

The more a person's study of body types broadens, the more it contributes to his understanding. He can begin to clarify for himself the loves he's had, and the ones that he hasn't, by applying what he knows about the attractions between types. Misunderstandings don't surprise him when he's been studying the subjective, idiosyncratic views of each type. He can even find the traits that might balance him, if he has an impulse toward self-improvement.

The ideas that lie within the study of body types have no trouble keeping pace with the variety of human activity. These ideas continue to fascinate the imagination, as they're fed by a constant stream of new observations. Whether scrutinizing the policies of an incumbent President or questioning the piety of a Renaissance Pope, knowing about types supercharges our comprehension, clarifies our thoughts and opens the door to an entirely new way of looking at people.

Someone who continues with this study may begin to glimpse the enneagram of types everywhere, like a complex and subtle symbolism underlying the whole fabric of society. Cataloging all the possibilities of this symbolism would certainly fill several books; maybe a few examples will reveal the scope of its influence.

Cycles of Beauty

Look at the way the ideal of beauty has oscillated over the centuries. Why is it so difficult today for many people to admire the robust and playful women in the paintings of Rubens? Perhaps the influence of each type, in turn, cycles through a period of dominance in society; if so, it may have swung away from these fleshy creatures. Today it is Saturn that rules our aesthetics. We may be living through one of the few ages of human history in which Saturnine women have been considered the epitome of feminine beauty, an age in which the dreams of millions of men have been populated by women who are aggressive, angular and vaguely masculine.

Or we could try to plot various roles in society on the plan of body types. Here the symbols of the types express the different kinds of work that men do, and which help to construct a varied, complete society. Lunar contributes persistent work and eccentricity; Venus is the type of growth, breeding and care; Mercury acts as a conduit for the intellect, and holds the edge of crime; Saturn stabilizes the whole and governs it; Mars wages war, guards the realm and pioneers new territories; Jovial teaches, amuses, heals and binds society together; Solar adds charisma and sparkle to the lot.

Types and Nations

Whole nations and races of people can be diagnosed according to this grammar of types. The long and insular history of the Chinese suggests they are a lunar race—secretive, willful and inscrutable. Or the history of the British, who have contributed to our ideas of fairness and justice while dominating whole continents: it's a picture of the type that stretches from Saturn to Mars. Or the inventive, quick and animated manner of the Japanese may put us in mind of dexterous Mercury.

On and on we could go, and the theory of body types would continue to spring at us from all directions. We can never use it up. Wandering over its vast and detailed landscape we're humbled, surprised and enlightened by turns, but we're never bored. Each observation, each understanding underscores the reality of types and propels us to more exact observations, deeper understandings.

Finally, we begin to grasp how potent and pervasive a tool we've inherited. It's a tool that achieves its greatest effect when it deepens our insight into ourselves, when it shows us quite new boundaries between the false and the real within us. That is when the outlines of the types emerge from the mists of wordy description, and begin to take on the familiar features of the world we have always lived within, but which we are only just beginning to see.

PART II

The Seven
Body Types

The Lunar Type

Lunar feelings, like still waters, run deep. A Lunar may be inwardly alive with excitement, but show others only the faintest blush. Those who have tried to open the secrets of a Lunar come away shaking their heads in frustration, sometimes in dismay. It seems that the more you want a Lunar to speak, the stronger his resistance becomes, and it can become perverse. Like the Cheshire cat in *Alice in Wonderland*, a Lunar can disappear just when you think he's about to tell you everything, and leave you with only a trace of his smile lingering in your mind.

Anyone who's had dealings with Lunars can tell you how they react to new ideas: they resist. But there's an accepted strategy for overcoming this problem, and that is to prepare yourself for 'no' as the first response to any request. And the second. The third time around you may find out how they actually feel; you've helped them work the 'no' out of their system.

Lunar Power

A Lunar's power isn't very hard to see: try telling him to do something he doesn't want to do. When he refuses, as he probably will, you'll see a negative form of power. It's not the power to make other people do what he wants, it's the power of an obstacle that can't be moved. But like all power, it's really about control.

Lunars' power is dedicated to not being controlled, just the way that more active forms of power are dedicated to controlling; avoiding a feeling of helplessness is the real concern for both. When active and passive forms of power meet, it may look like the irresistible force meeting the immovable object, but somehow, they exist for each other. Lunars need someone to refuse, to disobey, to ignore; they rely on more active types to rouse both their resistance, and the heady feeling of independence that comes with it. After they've denied you they can look at themselves and say, "You see, nobody forces me to do what I don't want; I cannot be moved by others." The fear of being taken advantage of, or being victimized, is strong enough to ensure that almost no one will get close to them.

This power has a positive side to it as well. When a Lunar has an aim he isn't easily distracted. He focuses on what he wants to do, and fortifies himself against anything that lies outside this narrow range. This persistence is an attractive trait of Lunar, and it's probably the best weapon Lunars have in their struggle to overcome a passivity so strong that it can make them numb.

A Passive, Negative Body Type

Lunar is a negative type, and Lunars are negative in an offhand, involuntary way. To them events are awful, people difficult, the job a bore and the outlook dim. So what can you expect? Without question, things will turn out poorly; in the meantime you can only sigh and get on with it. A Lunar is convinced that his efforts will end in failure or humiliation—and this certainty can keep him from committing himself. He feels that he's a person who is bound to fail, and this feeling darkens his entire view of the world.

When we're depressed, we tend to isolate ourselves, building psychological walls within which our dissatisfaction can ferment. Maybe it's this kind of barrier that alienates Lunars from the rest of us. They don't mix easily in society, and consider themselves outcasts, misunderstood and harried by more outgoing types. Their aloofness constricts them. Behind it lies both fear and the frustration of social paralysis. What is the fear? It is a fear of *exposure,* because being seen is what threatens; being seen brings unwanted attention, and behind this fear may lie a kind of shame. But to us, the same aloofness gives Lunars an air of mystery; they seem inscrutable, opaque.

This is a type that exaggerates its isolation in many ways. Lunars wear dark clothes that they hope will make them invisible, or at least, anonymous. Their humor is often childish, too simple, and somehow unfunny to anyone else. You'll see them giggling to themselves in the corners of rooms, where they can see anyone who's coming, and where, if they're lucky, they won't be noticed.

In the middle of a conversation they'll smirk at something you've said and, when pressed to tell you why, will confuse you with their explanation—there's just nothing funny in it. Lunars giggle at absurdities. They are the people you hear in dark movie houses laughing at all the poignant—or at all the wrong—places.

Uncomfortable in Society

It's not hard to see why Lunars meet so much resistance when they try to overcome this social problem. Their type lacks either an active part, or a positive one. Lunar is the only negative, passive body type, which can't be easy. They are so uncomfortable with social initiatives that their efforts to socialize sometimes turn them into supplicants, or sycophants, or lend them an abrupt, dismissive tone. They're too scared to be confident, and too wrapped in themselves to see the effect they're having. Without some jolt from necessity, or without a favorable circumstance, they slide back into inertia, go back behind the walls.

Lunars hide themselves, their ideas, and their activities more than any other type. They're not compelled, like others, to advertise themselves, and don't need your approval for motivation. Besides being naturally shy, they doubt you're interested in them anyway. A Lunar will suspect your motives if you show any interest in his life or his thoughts.

It's not just their bland personalities that make Lunars look colorless to others. They have a black-and-white view of the world—grey areas, confusion, and discrimination are tuned out of their picture. If it isn't right, it must be wrong. What isn't good has no ambiguity—it's simply bad. Moods carry them from one extreme to another, from childish expectation to depression, from persistent action to despair. You can't shake a Lunar out of his moods, and he can't either.

Rooted in Extremes

If Lunars are difficult to deal with it is because they've become rooted in these extremes, and their nature tells them not to budge. They get cantankerous and willful. Catch them in a mood like this and all your persuasion will only make them more rigid and unyielding.

Lunars' odd habits and strange manners may place them outside of consensus 'normality.' They look peculiar to us, but not to themselves, because they have their own curious logic to support them. All the types throw off an occasional eccentric, but Lunar is the only eccentric body type. His eccentricity somehow justifies his odd behavior and unique outlook to himself, but it can fuel his isolation as well.

We admire Lunars for their persistence, a never-quit approach to something once they've started. With their employer, their country or their ideas, this persistence seems like loyalty, and makes them tough and dependable. All the narrowness in their thinking then becomes constructive and makes them real supporters, tireless workers for the cause. On the pledge of their devotion you need never doubt— they'll be with you to the end.

Outside of Fashion

The Lunar is not a vibrant type, and they won't grab your attention in passing. The women have a doe-like look, and many don't want to attract attention. The men seem vulnerable, with a limpid sensitivity that can magnify the feminine element intrinsic to this type. When not dressed in black, they wear odd colors, in odd combinations. They like small, detailed prints, lace and ruffles. They give you the impression of being outside fashion, even if only by half-a-step. They can put together a chic look sometimes, but the effect is either too timid or too forceful, and you don't think they'll ever get it quite right.

Lunar beauty isn't much appreciated these days, even though the sculptures in which an attempt was made to carve a perfect female form, especially the Aphrodites of Greece, owe the type a great deal. We see in them the soft curves, delicate proportions and dewy skin of the ideal Lunar woman. No other type can approach the ideal Lunar's utterly perfect and feminine form. But in life, many Lunars inhabit odd and childish bodies. They seem unfinished, as if they were made of lumpy dough, or they have a cramped, owlish face and look old beyond their years.

Lunar and Saturn

It's easy to like Lunars; you want to protect them. Those tall, judicial types we frequently see them with are Saturns searching for someone to protect, someone to save. Saturns are the opposite of Lunars; they're active where Lunars are passive, masculine where Lunars are feminine, public where Lunars are private. Both Lunars and Saturns are lured to exactly what they themselves don't possess, and see in each other the material for their own completion. Like father and child, Saturn and Lunar create a stable atmosphere that reminds us of long-lasting family connections. It's not an atmosphere of passion and abandon.

Of course, this is a connection that easily unites Saturnine men with Lunar women. For a Saturn woman, on the other hand, Lunar men may seem baffling. They may be frightened by a Lunar's coolness, or frustrated by his inactivity. A Lunar's sweetness and quiet intimacy pull on deep needs of Saturn, but in the world of action Lunars often seem ineffectual and slow.

Cool and Detached

The coolness that so infuriates us in Lunars—their ability to ignore us completely, to remain aloof, to hide their feelings—also has another side. You'll see it in times of stress or danger when others may be tossed about by their emotions and reactions, and when Lunars remain composed, unmoved. Their natural restraint may keep them away from chatty parties, but it also puts them at a distance from the passions that overpower others.

This uncanny detachment opens the possibility of remarkable acts of selflessness and courage, like calmly walking into a burning room to carry out a trapped child.

This same certainty also surfaces in their conversations. A Lunar has already reduced his perceptions to extremes, a reduction that gives everything he says the heavy thud of fact, no matter how inane or eccentric his opinion may be. Whether right or wrong, he sounds right, and convinces people by this tone of infallibility.

A Medieval Connection

The Dark Ages give off a finicky Lunar air. When I think of the rigid ties of feudal serf to feudal lord, and the isolation of communities cut off from one another, I'm reminded of Lunar. It was an age that glorified God, but was overwhelmed by its own pessimism. Activity seems to have been very circumscribed, and life itself perpetually overcast. Even the darkness of the age reminds me of the subterranean air of Lunars, permanently turned away from society's light and the companionship of others. It even reminds me of the dark, invisible clothing they wear. In the medieval monasteries we get a glimpse of Lunar at work.

Imagine a monk bent over a manuscript in the scriptorium of some abbey and appreciate his humble dedication to the copying of old texts. This detailed, painstaking work, devoid of fame or recognition, seems to me one extreme example of Lunar's anonymous toil, and gives me a feeling for the age.

Study some of the medieval ivories, carved in religious devotion, or the intricate boxwood balls made by these monks, and you'll get this feeling too. Boxwood, dense and hard, can be worked to an extremely fine level of detail. I've seen one of these carvings in the Cloisters in New York, about the size of a baseball. In it you see a vast panorama; the countryside in the foreground gives way to a cityscape in the background, where merchants, soldiers and holy processions compete for space. In the fields the peasants toil, and in the city individual buildings are microscopically described. No matter how hard you look, you can't find those spots where the particular breaks down and gives way to the texture of the wood itself.

There's a touch of lunacy here. A low but insistent whisper of madness and confusion echoes in your mind when you try to figure out the motives, let alone the methods, of the artists who created such puzzles. This uncanny and self-sacrificing devotion strikes me as an emblem of Lunar.

Finding Lunars Today

In more modern times, Lunars use the same abilities and dedication that the medieval monks used, but in research, or in libraries where they patiently study and work alone. They are anonymous and diligent back-office workers, precise and confident with books and numbers, and make excellent accountants and librarians. They squint in the light of publicity or acclaim, and can't wait to return to the solitude of their studies. Lost in the smallest parts of their subject, Lunars rely on others to work out the implications of what they've found. Their infatuation is with breaking things down, discerning smaller and smaller quantities to be named, analyzed and related, not in building up a view of the whole.

The Lunar Type in Art

The paintings of the seventeenth-century Dutch painter Jan Vermeer often remind me of Lunar—especially those of lonely or isolated women, serene in some corner of their home. These women have a beautiful softness, or a childish reserve that's Lunar. From up close the studied detail of rugs draped over tables, or the clarity of maps tacked to the walls, is dazzling. The whole scene is distant, separated from us forever by an invisible detachment. The people in these paintings don't invite us to share the moment that's been captured here, but remain self-absorbed, untouchable.

The landscapes of Jean-Baptiste Camille Corot give me another insight into Lunar. These pastoral scenes are delicately colored, hazy and poignant. We want to watch the world from here, protected by the deep shade of an overhanging tree, and have no desire to venture out into the light.

Odd Personal Traits

Lunars, like nocturnal animals, populate late-night cities and can be observed slinking quietly down deserted streets, or staring out from behind the counter of an all-night coffee shop. They seem to embody a more primitive life, one in which it was only safe in the cave, and darkness hid the dangers of the day.

A Lunar's home can give you a subterranean chill. Pull aside the drapes that cover a window in his dimly lit room and you may be in for a surprise. You're just as apt to discover a fantastic view as you are to find yourself looking down an airshaft; he just doesn't care about what's outside. He would rather arise late in the day to a cool, darkened den.

Lunars put me in mind of owls or ferrets or, occasionally, rabbits; mostly creatures that live close to the ground. Their ability to survive among larger, more powerful predators stirs my admiration for their persistence and self-reliance. Lunars are tough, it's true, and shot through with stubbornness. But besides their timidity, they have an innocence that makes them endearing, and that prompts a tenderness in the rest of us that is truly their own.

The Lunar Type

General Orientation:
Passive-Feminine / Negative

Psychological Overview:
Chief Feature of willfulness or aloofness
Maximum attraction of Saturn
Maximum repulsion of everyone, but particularly other negative types.

Key Words:
Eccentric, inscrutable, pessimistic, secretive, wary, uncommunicative, unemotional, fearful

Examples:

Meg Tilly	Emily Dickinson
Woody Allen	Truman Capote
Harry Truman	Tom Wolfe
Andy Warhol	

William Benham's Physical Description:

The Lunar is tall in stature, fleshy in build, with the lower limbs thick and the feet large. He is often quite stout, but his flesh is not firm and his muscles are not strong. He is soft and flabby and instead of muscular vitality, his flesh has a spongy feeling. His complexion is dead white, giving him a decided pallor and marking him as the victim of a weak heart's action, anemia, kidney trouble.

His head is round, thick through the temples, bulging over the eyes and with a low forehead. The hair is not thick, but straggly and fine in quality, brows are scanty, uneven in contour, and often grow together over the nose. The eyes are round and 'starey' in appearance, often bulging, and frequently watery. The color is gray or light blue, the whites are clear, and the pupil has a luminous appearance, seeming to refract light and showing a prismatic gleam. The lids are thick and flabby, giving them a swollen look. The nose is short and small, quite often turning up at the end, and sometimes showing the nostrils very plainly. Frequently it is what we call a 'pug' nose.

The mouth is small, and puckers, giving the appearance of being drawn together. The teeth are large and long, yellow in color, and irregularly placed in the gums, which are prominent and bloodless-looking. The teeth are soft and decay early. The chin is heavy, hanging in flabby folds and receding. The neck is fleshy, flabby, and wrinkled, connecting this peculiar-looking head with the fleshy-looking chest, which is again flabby and spongy in consistency. The voice is thin and pitched often in high key. The ears are small and set close to his head. The abdomen is large and bulges forward, giving an awkward look, and the legs are not graceful, but thick and heavy, having a dropsical appearance. The feet are flat and large and the gait is a shuffle or is shambling, very much like the gait of a sailor when he walks on land.

Lunar Circulation

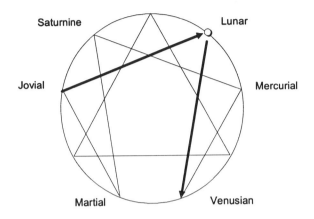

From Coolness to Growth

Coming from Jovial, the Lunar retains some residual interest in people, but it is not overtly expressed. This interest dies in Lunar, as the energy of the type sinks into the 'slough of despond' and activity reaches its nadir. Moving through the depths of Lunar, hopefulness begins to make a dim appearance, and the intimations of Venus soften the despair of Lunar.

In moving toward Venus, Lunars can counteract many of the negative traits that defeat them, particularly in their relations with others. Trapped within a cool exterior and seemingly aloof, Lunars can be softened by the smoldering warmth of Venus. Lunar rigidity is modulated by Venusian ease. However, to maximize the growth inherent in this circulation, Lunars must be careful to not lose the strength of persistence in the midst of what may seem an inviting

Venusian sloth, or lose the strength of their focus in Venusian diffusion and non-existence. The paralysis of inattention may strike the Lunar, who is already passive but may have Venusian inertia to deal with as well. It is only by combining strengths, and agreeing to give up a small amount of the feeling of being 'special,' that the Lunar circulation to Venus becomes truly evolutionary.

Lunar–Venusian

This type may be the most passive on the enneagram, merging Lunar quiet with Venusian passivity. Lunar-Venusian can be seen as a softer Lunar, or perhaps a cool Venusian. The maximum attraction is naturally Saturn-Mars, the most active of types.

Lunar-Venusians will have great difficulty making up their minds or taking any kind of decisive action. They may find themselves trapped between inertia and sloth, and have little force to move out of difficult situations. On the other hand, Lunar-Venusian is a particularly soft and feminine type, and may radiate warmth in a quiet, contained manner. Their focus on home and family matters make them ideally suited to roles around the home.

Examples:

Aphrodite	Helena Bonham-Carter
Woodrow Wilson	Jimmy Carter
Queen Elizabeth II	Kevin MacReynolds

The Venusian Type

Like Lunar, Venusian is passive and feminine. However, Venusian is positive and receptive where Lunar is negative and inaccessible, and it is this combination of traits that dominates Venusians, and that gives them their tone.

Venusians seem to be able to accept almost anyone, no matter how lame, ill or ugly they might be. Any living thing can grab hold of their attention, and the more that help is needed, the more strongly will a Venusian respond. The complete lack of judgment that makes this uncritical aid possible is one of the Venusian's most attractive traits.

Close to Nature

Venus displays the same rude equality as the world of nature does. Venusians don't choose one person over another; they accommodate everyone. They are generous, open and undiscriminating, which makes them attractive to all. But sometimes they are *too* open, *too* undiscriminating, and then it becomes something else.

Generosity demands that we surrender a bit of ourselves for someone else's good. But how much can we give before we start to cut into what we are, the sources of our identity? Most of us have a clear idea of this boundary, and get wary when we're near it. We resist what we think will blur the outlines of our identity, and pull back.

Character Becomes Blurred

Venusians aren't as worried, or perhaps they don't have as clear an image of themselves as others do. Discrimination seems like cruelty to them, and the contour of their character blurs as they surrender home, clothes, time and attention to anyone who asks. They will give up their own interests in favor of yours. They'll let the subject you introduce in a conversation interrupt their own, and may not even notice. They think less of their opinions than anyone else does, and demand little from their friendships. Their dreams of glory most often put them next to someone famous; not in the spotlight, but in its shadow.

Falling into 'Non-existence'

Their own goodness victimizes them. When a Venusian gives up his own desires or his own thoughts, he may be giving up his own individuality at the same time. He shies away from asserting himself, and doesn't want to make decisions. His slide into passivity robs him of the clearly defined character that other types get from exercising their personalities. Being too accepting saps his force and dilutes his very considerable warmth. Whatever he says or does lacks force, and doesn't stick. You might say that he has *ceased to exist*.

You won't find a Venusian alone much—he wilts in isolation. Sitting apart, his already smooth, featureless face tends to go slack. He's flaccid when there's no one else around to stimulate his own vitality. He prefers a mob crowding around, and the warmth of all those bodies. In seclusion he can't find anything to do with himself, and gets panicked by having to make the most ordinary decisions; should he do the laundry first, or should he go shopping?

This type has an incessant need for contact; not affection, but proximity. Like a pet you've grown accustomed to, you're likely to find them snuggled next to you, their shoulder on yours, hips touching. They'll coerce you into all the hugs and kisses, pats and cuddles you can stand—and more—to get some energy they don't seem to generate themselves. They're always attaching themselves to one host or another, like creeping vines, or bright-faced bougainvillaea, climbing up you to get the sunshine they need. Or maybe they're trying to speed up their lagging metabolism. They are, of all the types, the slowest.

Any Venusian may suddenly ask you for a massage, or offer to give you one. Saturns have this habit too, but in their case it's simply another way they may be able to improve you. Venusians want to make you feel better, and they want to get all that fleshy contact that goes with the job.

Unconditional Acceptance

One of the keys to their universal popularity is that you don't have to be interested in what they did today; they're happy if you're just in the room with them. Where else will you find someone who's glad to feed you, happy to touch you, eager for the details of your triumphs and stumbles? Someone who won't bore you with his own stories, or interrupt you to disagree with your opinion? Only with a Venusian. Why shouldn't they be popular?

Venusians get us to confide in them, and tell them all our deepest secrets. It's surprising how easy and confident a Venusian can make us feel. We gladly confess the most humiliating incidents of our lives when faced with their benign acceptance. Since they don't compete with us, don't begrudge our wider fields of interest, it scarcely matters that they also don't need to understand us. No matter how stupid or inept we're feeling, no matter how frequent our social gaffes, it only takes a Venusian nearby to dissolve our self-judgment with warmth and acceptance.

A Healing Quality

Venusians are detached in their generosity, almost indifferent. They're concerned with so many people that individuals don't matter to them as much as we might think. Their hunger is for people on whom to lavish their care; they attract whichever 'victims' will feed this need. Oddly enough, it's this indifference that's partly responsible for the comfort they bring us; we know we're not being judged for our flaws, and we're able to accept ourselves. We feel cleansed, healed, self-confident again, and back on our feet.

Lack of Focus

The more you study Venusians the more clearly you see this lack of independence—and lack of focus—in them. They weigh heavily on the people to whom they attach themselves. By converting the ideas and concerns of a friend, teacher or mate into their own concerns, they attempt to shine by the light reflected there, a satellite glowing but cold. The energy they draw off their host is food for the life on the surface of their personality, and it's food that they can't do without.

You can count on getting a friendly reception from a Venusian no matter how long it's been since you last saw him. Walk in on an old friend like this and he'll only want

84

to put you at your ease, make you as happy as he is. He'll still be as loyal as an old dog, and as comfortable as your bedroom slippers.

A Sensuous Type

It's important to a Venusian to feel comfortable. They want clothes that are loose and cozy, that feel good. They like touching and being touched. They run their hands over the furniture, caress the vegetables in the sink and curl up with their pets, or children, for frequent naps. It takes something stimulating their senses to make them feel alive. They can't cook without sticking their fingers in the food, and they get a look of bliss when they're up to their elbows in dough, or mashing the potatoes through their fingers.

Sensuality propels Venusian eroticism, not passion, or lust. It's the warmth of the body that they love, its textures and smells. They are not trying to conquer you with sex, like some types, nor do they try to transcend their own personality, like others. They use sex for its sensuality, its closeness; it's a natural joy they get, like a child's, and it doesn't put us off.

Venusians in Art

Painters have capitalized on this sensuality. Venusians lounge in a languorous mist of sated passions on cushions and divans in the art of many periods. They're frank and open, gazing at us with a proud look of unabashed sensuality. Their ample femininity finds its way into paintings of famous erotics and lovers, whether gazing as expectantly as Danaë, or with the casual, dismissive glance of an odalisque. Titian, for example, fashions their bodies into satiny boudoir pillows. François Boucher makes them look as if they've been de-boned, leaving only enough of a skeleton to keep the moist flesh suspended, trembling.

Venusians give off a humid air of sensuality and remind us of the steamy earthiness of the Mediterranean world whether they come from Venice or Vancouver. The thick, dark hair on many Venusians' bodies—both men and women—heightens this impression. The sensuality that makes them artistic and intuitive lovers is as natural a force as the tides, and as regular. They're free from many of the insecurities and fears that cloud others' enjoyment of life's physical pleasures.

The World of Sensations

Venusians get a simple, animal pleasure from their senses. They surround sex with a luxurious mist of sensation. And yet they can get caught up in sensuality and become victimized by it, all too easily swept away in a rush of sensations. Their emotions then have little play exactly where they are most needed; they've been pushed into the background by earthier drives. The balance that the mind can bring, being more fragile, has already vanished.

The Power of Passivity

Venusians wield the power of passivity. The strength that they have comes from constancy, and through it Venusians overcome stronger, but more cyclical forces. From classical ages Venus is shown as the conqueror of Mars, her lover and adversary, through this power. Mars may rage with passion, but he can't last forever. Artists show us the war god who, having fought the noble fight in Venus' arms, has reached the end of his energy. There he lies, pitifully, spent and at

Venus' feet. The radiant goddess looks on—sometimes with a smirk.

By a similar method Venusians exert a considerable force on people and events, but it's a force that's difficult to gauge. Their steady pressure can smother you even though it appears benevolent. It's the same way a growing tree that provides you with shade and beauty can bring down your house by growing right through the walls. The strength in this process may surprise you when it rises to the surface from beneath a Venusian's slow and gentle personality—what's surprising is that it feels so inevitable.

A Passive Form of Power

We're used to seeing power in explosive, compelling acts, and are unprepared for the resolve that lies beneath a Venusian's passivity. You'd think a type as passive as Venus would be easily distracted by the powerful currents of life, thrown by more active people. But it isn't always true; Venusians just have a longer view, which gives them more time to get their way.

Slow, natural growth rules many of a Venusian's activities. Thriving plants may crowd their homes and contribute to the relaxed, messy ambiance. Somehow it's not surprising to find a Venusian cooing to the cucumbers in his garden, or encouraging his coleus to take its medicine. He doesn't doubt his ability to communicate with either kids or trees by way of some instinctive language no one else is able to decipher.

In the city you'll find Venusians mooning over their flower boxes, and in the suburbs they're out planting bushes, or in the pay of a landscaper. Plants need the regular care that comes so easily to Venusians, and pull on their affections like members of the family.

Steady Homebodies

Home and household exert a powerful pull on Venusians. They can often raise children as competently as they grow plants. They like the close connections built into family life, and the nurturing it requires. A family gives them something to belong to, and a whole crowd to look after. Their children don't lack for love, or for reassurance; they're more likely to be smothered by affection than driven by ambition. Venusians forgive their children everything, trying to heal with warmth what others might correct with discipline.

Venusians don't often get restless. They've already got a job, so why look for another? Their apartment isn't so great, but it's more comfortable than moving. They feel safe with

familiar things and don't need the excitement of an unknown city, a new career or a dangerous adventure to make their blood run faster. They get high on people, on animals, on the shared reliance of a social mob. Their roots go deep into the loamy soil of their lives, and aren't easily or painlessly transplanted. They shrug off the thirst for exotic, strange or uncomfortable experiences that animates more difficult types, and find satisfaction curled up in their favorite overstuffed chair, where everything's within easy reach.

Recognizing Venusian

Venusians pay a price for being so easily satisfied. Sometimes they give me the feeling that they were created quickly, without sharp corners or a detailed finish; they were never brought into focus. They present us with a pleasant but hazy profile; the people you can't remember from a party, or whose face never connects with a name. They are the kids that get forgotten when sides are being chosen, but don't let it get in the way of their loyalty.

In a group they'll smile and nod, and don't mind being interrupted. They're looking for someone to agree with, not for a fight. Venusians see the logic in everyone's arguments, but have little to offer of their own, besides support. They'd like everyone to get along and have a good time. The principles for which some people will take a stand, risking a rancorous attention, just don't seem that important.

The Limits of Naïveté

Naïveté accompanies all this goodness, and may blind Venusians to the squalor and infamy of life. Instead of trusting, they become gullible, and get teased by everyone. Naïveté makes them an easy mark for con men and fiery preachers. They are charged with their desire to belong, and hold firm to their belief in everyone's goodness. Ignorant of the dark motives of manipulators they allow their own interests to get squeezed out, and find that they've been used.

Venusians adopt the logic of a cause without worrying about its deeper ambiguities. They willingly become devotees, and in the unfortunate event that they're abused for it, still won't rebel against their manipulators. It's sad but common to see a Venusian determined to rehabilitate the salesman who's just swindled an outrageous sum of money out of him. He thinks this wretch is himself a victim who would come to his senses if he only received enough care; any defects the Venusian finds in a greedy or criminal personality he is sure can be cured by applying great dollops of sweetness and understanding.

Are They Too Relaxed?

Venusians lack the tautness of a well-defined character. There's no tension to give force to their personality, and little tone to their actions. They aren't compelled to have opinions, or convert you to their way of thinking. Browbeating them won't do any good—it only confuses their efforts to please you. They'll express an opinion if you like, but they're just as willing to abandon it if necessary for one that's more popular. The contradictions that force us to struggle to a unique understanding have little affect on Venusians, who really excel at staying relaxed and loose in all situations.

This general lack of tone strikes deep into their lives and makes their bodies soft, their habits slothful and their minds inert. You'll find a Venusian laying on his couch, food scattered around, everything a bit mussed. He's at home with the entropy of his little universe, and doesn't see much reason to do anything about it; after all, it's natural. Mention to him the clothes he's got on, or point to the tracks his dinner left as it toppled down his dressing gown, and he's mildly surprised; he hadn't noticed.

This may be the only type that can leave the house wearing unmatched socks, or a dress inside out, and when it's mentioned be neither particularly astonished, nor too upset by the lapse. Venusians float through their day in something of a muddle, and no matter how much they spend on clothes always seem poorly put together. Within five minutes a Venusian can make a shirt fresh from the store look comfortable; give him ten minutes, and it will be positively rumpled.

Difficulties Arise from Passivity

Their sloth, passivity, and unfocused geniality create profound difficulties for Venusians. They slide easily into a vacant space inside themselves that feels both comatose and secure. Pressure will drive them to this space, or stress, or fatigue. Watch them in front of the television, at the movies or over dinner. If they think no one is looking, their eyes glaze over, their mouths fall slightly open, their muscles go limp.

In this state there are no opinions, no desires, no thoughts, and no responsibilities. Everything that's unique, unusual, interesting—all the idiosyncracies that might make them truly human—slip away. Personality has vanished and taken their individuality along with it, even while you watch. Only the body remains behind. They're on hold, in neutral, something like the blank but active screen of a TV test pattern.

It's in this state that Venusians become victims. They defend themselves against violence, injustice and ill-will by surrendering their existence. Wrapping themselves in a void of not knowing, not caring, they hope it has made them invulnerable by making them invisible. They look for sanctuary from their faults and from the wrongs of the world by tuning in to some private void for a while. They want to rid themselves of whatever is objectionable by the same method.

It's a poor defense, and self-defeating; it leaves a Venusian nothing with which to fight, nothing with which to gather his strength. He descends naturally into oblivion—it's a habit. When he snaps back, he may not even know what's happened. You have to fill him in like an amnesiac who occasionally loses track of time.

Strength of Loyalty

Venusian loyalty strengthens the web of society. They support social groups of all kinds from companies to frat houses to local churches. Reliability strengthens them, and allows them to contribute their support and care. Venusians gravitate to the healing professions; they become exemplary doctors, nurses and caregivers. They get a charge from food, and cook creatively. They like to work in an office where they don't have to move around too much, but sometimes fall into rough and dangerous jobs when they try to fabricate an active personality, or imitate their opposite type, the Martial.

Although we can be put off by Venusians when they are hazy or indistinct, they endear themselves to us by their supple generosity, their healing warmth and their genuine kindness. Venusians confront a formidable task when they try to change their nature and its habitual responses. But they dull the harshness of the world for the rest of us, and ease our progress through life.

The Venusian Type

General Orientation:
Passive-Feminine / Positive

Psychological Overview:
Chief Features of non-existence, sloth
Maximum attraction of Mars
No *maximum repulsion;* doesn't care enough, or simply
avoids problems with other people.

Key Words:
Growth, earthbound, family-oriented, low self-esteem
(non-existence), malleable, uncommunicative

Examples:

Willard Scott	Marilyn Monroe
Jackie Gleason	Roseanne Arnold

William Benham's Physical Description:

In appearance the Venusian is attractive and beautiful. He is graceful, shapely, well balanced and easy in his manner, presenting more a type of feminine beauty than masculine. The Solar and Jovial are types of manly beauty, the male Venusian partakes of the soft voluptuousness of female beauty. These subjects are of medium height, and present graceful curves of form from head to foot. The skin is white, fine in texture, soft and velvety to the touch, transparent in its fineness, through which a delicate pink color glows, showing normal health and blood supply. The face is round or oval in shape, is finely proportioned, with no high cheek bones, thin cheeks, prominent temples, or square jaws to make it angular or mar its beauty. The cheeks are well rounded, and often show dimples when the face breaks into a smile. The forehead is high, well proportioned, gracefully rounding in front, perfect in contour. The skin on the forehead is tightly drawn, and does not wrinkle, nor do crows'-feet appear at the corners of the eyes in young subjects. These come later in life and after Venusian fires have fiercely burned. There is a Venusian mark on the forehead which is seen in young Venusians, which consists of three vertical wrinkles over the bridge of the nose between the eyes. The hair is abundant, long and wavy. The Venusian does not grow bald naturally; when so found it is from some unnatural cause. The eyebrows are well marked, abundant, and form graceful curves on the forehead, well pointed at the ends, sharply outlined, and seldom growing over the nose. The eyes are round or almond-shaped, brown or dark blue in color, and have a tender expression of human sympathy. When the passions are aroused they have a voluptuous expression which it is impossible to mistake. The Venusian is a fine subject—in his whole physical make-up this fineness of texture shows constantly; his eyelids are smooth in quality, with delicately traced blue veins showing through, and with long silky lashes curling upward on the ends. The nose is shapely, full sized, but with fine curves. The nostrils are broad, and show varying moods by their rapid contraction or expansion when the subject is excited.

The mouth is beautifully shaped, with bow-like curves and full, red lips, the lower one slightly more prominent. The teeth are white, medium in size, strong, and set in beautifully colored, healthy-looking gums; so when the Venusian smiles—the dimpled cheeks, the expressive eyes, the white teeth showing through full red lips, and set in pink gums—make a most attractive picture. The chin is round and full, often dimpled on the end, and completes the graceful contour of the face. The neck is long, full, and shapely, connecting the well-shaped head with gracefully drooping shoulders, which, while they do not speak of muscular strength, show breadth and health. The chest is large, full, round, and expansive, thus giving the lungs full play. The voice is full, musical, and attractive. It shows no weakness in tone, and yet has not the Martian strength. The legs are graceful in shape, the hips high

and round, even in male Venusians, and the thigh propor-
tionately long. The feet are small and shapely, with a high-ar-
ched instep, which gives him grace and elasticity in his walk.
Altogether, the Venusian is refined, graceful, lovable, and
attractive, the most apt figure to fill the very sphere in life for
which he was intended, by adding brightness, joy, gay spirits,
and love to a world without which selfishness and monotony
would surely rule. The hand of the Venusian is white, soft,
fine in texture, pink in color, fingers of medium length or
short, tips conic, slightly square or of a small, spatulate shape,
nails filbert and pink, thumb medium or small, and a large
Mount of Venus either smooth or grilled.

Venusian Circulation

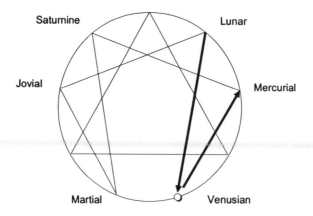

From Warmth to Wit

Venusian contains within it traces of both the fading femininity of Lunar before it, and the rising masculinity of Mercury, ahead of it on the enneagram. Venusian sensuality may be influenced from either direction, as well, with Lunar providing a quiet but possibly dark sensuality, and Mercury lending an active, playful side.

Moving toward Mercury, Venusians can see the correction for their lack of self-image in the energy that Mercuries give to their appearance, and the attention they lavish on self; self-image, self-confidence, and so on. This self-interest and the greater physical and mental activity associated with Mercury can cure the Venusian's passivity and self-deprecation, the two traits that may be their most worrisome.

In this progression, it is important for Venusians to avoid the vanity and self-absorption that weaken the Mercury. The attractive traits that they seek ought to be acquired without taking on all the rest of the Mercury's baggage. Venusians are apt to become overly concerned with self as a reaction to their former *laissez-faire* attitudes, and may try to force their opinions on others in an attempt to overcome their non-existence.

Venus–Mercury

The combination of Venus sensuality and Mercurial playfulness creates a type that is attractive to many others. The lithe frame of Mercury is softened by the earthiness of Venus. It is a type ideally suited to acting, to disguise of any kind, and may find it a little too easy to deceive others.

Facile talkers with the ability to put others immediately at ease, Venus-Mercuries are ideal spokespeople, salespeople, representatives. If weighted toward Venus, they will enjoy home life, and if toward Mercury, they feel most comfortable among friends and in social situations.

There are many contradictions between these two types that create internal struggles for anyone that combines them both. For instance, the Venus side of a Venus-Mercury may hate to offend anyone, but the Mercury side can be utterly insensitive. Or the Venus may spend as much time as possible 'hanging out,' only to have the Mercury leap up and engage in frenetic activity. As each waxes and wanes in influence, these differences can make life quite challenging, and present many of the themes that will occupy a lifetime of inner work.

Examples:

Elizabeth Taylor	Al Pacino
Bob Costas	Elvis Presley
Debra Winger	Dustin Hoffman
Eddie Murphy	Michael Dukakis

The Mercurial Type

As we leave Venus we move into the realm of the active, or masculine, body types. Mercury, a negative type, is the first, followed by Saturn and Mars. Mercury combines the active and the negative in quite a different way than does Mars, the other active, negative type. Both can be self-interested and manipulative, but in distinct and different ways. While Mercury schemes, Mars attacks; where Mercury is devious, Mars is likely to be blunt and brutal. Each of them can influence other people with ease, but use opposing styles to do so. You may be bullied by a Martial, but a Mercury will trick you with his charming and convincing tone. Speed and perceptiveness are what typify Mercury.

Loves the Spotlight

You won't have any trouble locating Mercuries, because they want to be seen. Restless, quick and inquisitive, they love the spotlight. Everything about a Mercury—curly hair, small frame, finely made hands and feet, and distinct features—is perpetually moving. He has the agility of an athlete, the animation of an actor, and all his roles are active ones—at least in his imagination. Indeed, a Mercury's relation to life may become like that of an actor to his script, as he struts and frets his imagined hour upon the stage of life.

Mercuries dress for effect and can positively glitter in this effort to attract attention. They always feel as though they, and they alone, exist at center stage. Each scene in their life crashes into the next, and drama seems to be everywhere. Their eyes flick back and forth constantly, keeping track of all the reactions around them, like an insecure speaker worried about losing his audience. Mercuries have the thespian's flourishes to match their attitudes, and a deep voice that surprises you when it comes rolling out of such a small body. When they get 'turned on' they're devious and cunning, constantly hatching plots, or confidentially hissing asides to let us in on their complicated schemes.

With a passion for fame, and a lust to be known, Mercuries have no difficulty standing out in a crowd. They announce their skills, like an abbreviated résumé, apparently without the self-consciousness that you or I might feel. But they are watching for your response; do you admire their excellence as profoundly as they do themselves? And here is where Mercuries get caught in a paradox made of their own suspicions combined with their need for approval: they won't trust your affection if you don't approve of them, but they won't trust your judgment if you do. They know it's all an act; why can't you see it? And if you do see it, they're gone, because they do not want to be found out.

Always on Stage

Every Mercury has a bit of the orator, the actor, the revolutionary in him. Like them, he's endlessly selling. And he's a terrific salesman, persuading us with his charm, his wit and his sparkling eyes; it's not his sincerity we prize him for.

A Mercury's wit flashes quickly and it can be sharp. He may use his genius at mimicry to become a marvelous mime. Only his yen for approval, and his constant need to be liked, tarnish this otherwise admirable presentation.

Although Mercuries entertain us with their wit and cheer us with their sunniness, it's just as easy for them to suspect us of treason, or take a dark and apocalyptic view of their own future. Despite their outward radiance, their distrust and pessimism reveal the darker sides of a negative body type.

A Wish to Manipulate

Lunars also are negative, but passively. For instance, they dig in their heels when pushed, but are compliant if left alone. Mercuries don't wait for someone to set them off. They have plans to actualize and methods for getting what they want. While the lengths to which they're willing to go for their ambitions differ as much as individuals and their private motives differ, Mercuries itch to rule the people and events that appear necessary to their aims, or who just happen to be there, bystanders the Mercury believes are simply waiting for someone to tell them what to do.

For some Mercuries, the desire for control that underlies many of their aspirations can itself become their chief desire, guarded zealously by a habitual, vast and consistent suspicion.

A Suspicious Type

Perceptiveness joined to suspicion nudges Mercuries towards paranoia. They despise victims, and dread becoming—or being perceived—as a victim themselves. They stay alert for the plots they know exist, and are constantly trying to ferret out some iota of information that might save them from their own anxiety.

103

They pick up tidbits of information the rest of us would find meaningless, or banal. Questions asked by a Mercury have the uncomfortable edge of an interrogation, in which what you say—or the tone of your voice, or the way you hold your drink—is no longer trivial, and may be used against you. A Mercury can make you wonder if you've said too much, or not enough, to have justified your existence.

Since even a Mercury doesn't know all his own needs or all the motives that drive him, he may be right to be suspicious; it is a perceptive type, and maybe he's seen something we've simply missed. But after an exchange like this, we'll be uncertain about his charges, and equally unable to believe them.

All this suspicion makes for a treacherous journey through life. Mercuries are convinced that there is some nameless, capricious force that may have mined their road with pitfalls, perhaps just waiting to spring a few clever traps. Their deepest fear is the fear of losing control. Nothing makes them more edgy than a situation in which they have no say, or one in which they have to obey the orders issued to them. They see in these predicaments the certainty of being treated unfairly, or being rudely victimized. To protect themselves they demand that their rights and responsibilities be pointed out to them.

Mercuries study rules, laws and regulations, and can sniff out loopholes no one has seen before. They can't stand the idea that someone found a better buy on a car, or made a more profitable marriage. Although they don't trust what you tell them, they'll still worry about what you haven't told them, and wonder why you're holding out.

They can't imagine that anyone else is concerned for their benefit, only for their downfall. One of the principles that guides a Mercury through life is the belief that everyone is acting from self-interest. This he never doubts, and will accuse his boss, a friend, or his own mother of scheming against him. Nothing delights a Mercury more than having gotten a better deal than you did; when you're naïve about his motives his childish glee at getting the better of you seems adorable.

One way you might experience this overriding suspicion is by giving a Mercury a gift. You can almost see the wheels turning as he tries to figure out what you paid for it, and what you're going to ask for in return. He may be sure he deserves your generosity for being such a wonderful guy; he may even be thrilled because he got something for free; but the anxiety you've caused makes him lose his poise. In his world, there are no simple actions, and he assumes that everyone's motives are obscure.

Assaulted by suspicion, Mercuries become circumspect and wary. They have difficulty trusting their friends or confiding in their mates. Their quick minds may well be several steps ahead of yours, but rampant uncertainties shake their confidence. They are never quite sure of the value of their own perceptions. So many things seem possible to a Mercury, he can't commit himself completely. Instead, racing here and there to hedge his bets, he tries to cover every eventuality.

Intellectually Active

Complexity doesn't daunt them, however, the way it might addle you or I. Rather than resenting it, Mercuries make good use of complexity. It's their quick control over intricate arguments and their command of jargon that make conversation thrilling for a Mercury, and safe. Whether the subject is politics or poetry, he charges ahead, convinced you'll never be able to keep up. He covers his tracks, flings clouds of obscurities to keep you from finding out his secrets. Complexity becomes a drug he uses to keep away the curious, who may wish him harm, and the simple, whom he disdains.

Of course, from one point of view their suspicions are on target: after all, there are a lot of other Mercuries out there, and no telling what schemes they're hatching right now.

Traces of the Criminal

It would be absurd to say that Mercuries are criminal, because crime belongs to individuals, not to categories of people. But it is also true that there is no other type in which certain kinds of crime find so little resistance. Petty misdemeanors are habitual. They come home with pens from the office or tools from the shop, without realizing they've made off with someone else's property. Sidewalk stands present goods for the taking, if you're keen enough not to be caught. It's a morality that rewards their speed, their circumspection and, above all, their cleverness.

You could say that this is another example of the childish side of Mercury, where moral and ethical concerns don't carry the same weight they do for more mature types. Maybe it's the elasticity of their morals that's on display. It's certainly a convenience—even a luxury—for a Mercury to have such flexible principles. He must have a great deal of faith in them, because no one else's principles seem to stretch quite as far as a Mercury's, nor quite as easily.

I admire the assurance and optimism of Mercuries, perhaps because I neither organize nor advertise myself as rigorously as they. They always progress on schedule, no matter how often the schedule needs to be changed. If you attempt to pin them down, you'll get a chance to watch them wriggle and squirm their way off your hook. If they couldn't keep their options open, their plans fluid and their movement unhindered, they would be miserable.

Enjoy Being 'Serviceable'

Mercuries are useful in so many ways that it's a surprise when they resent their own utility. They're usually first to volunteer for a project, and quick to offer their opinions. Mercuries delight you by anticipating your needs. They arrange activities, recruit participants, and entertain everyone effortlessly; you'd think they'd be proud of the service. But their fantasies revolve around pulling the strings, not being pulled.

Saturns and Jovials make a Mercury nervous. He assumes the Saturn is there to look over his shoulder, and is going to limit his field of activity. He suspects the Jovial is humoring him. Either is disconcerting, but not nearly as much as being ignored; it's the only action he can't forgive. It's better to find some way to communicate with him, even if it's caustic, because if you disregard him or his concerns you are going to make an enemy. Then he'll get your attention for sure.

A Love of Entertaining

Entertaining is natural for Mercuries, and they're electric amongst their company, working the crowd, sincere and confidential no matter whom they're talking to. They love to correct you, but aren't actually interested in hanging around for the conversation to ripen; they never have time with so many people to see. They relish dressing up, and frequently appear in what may look like a costume. They use these costumes to create dramatic entrances and exits, and as disguises to obscure their plans, their intents or their identity. You'll often see Mercurial men sporting a neat moustache or beard, which not only adds to the show but helps them overcome that embarrassingly youthful look they maintain, even late into life.

A Mercury's youthfulness announces itself in many ways. He looks the youngest of all the types and his age may surprise you. Although he's in a rush to grow up, and has an adolescent's prickly sensitivity to anyone who doesn't take him seriously enough, the pranks, teasing, tantrums and innocence of childhood never really leave him.

As children Mercuries are manipulative and precocious. Their sunny dispositions and passion for approval make them bright and ready to please. Sparkling eyes and a quick wit delight us, too, and their resonant voices can arouse us like no one else's can. They're fun to be with, and enjoy life at a trot.

The Fastest Body Type

Their thoughts race along at the same speed that their moods change. A spitting rage will descend on them in a

moment, and then blow over like summer clouds, the day sunny again. A Mercury is an impulsive creature, rash and heady for action, always ready to go and itching with impatience at any delay. His attention flickers from one subject to the next, never lingering long before setting out on a new course. His restlessness comes from an overactive mind, and from the durability of his dissatisfaction.

These restless impulses compel Mercuries to take charge of projects with enthusiasm. They can often be found organizing, innovating, filling all sorts of active roles with confidence. Their activity is joined to a lithe masculinity. Mercuries are quite capable of sliding into a more passive role, and have no difficulty acting the victim. Their masculinity doesn't get in the way of playing this role as long as there's an advantage to be gained, and Mercuries certainly have enough complaints to sustain it. Perhaps they'll get something through your sympathy, and they don't particularly care what tools it takes to get it.

Mercurials in Shakespeare

Two of Shakespeare's most interesting villains shed light on the Mercurial type. Iago offers an extreme. All his weaknesses are blown to distortion, and all his strengths have been bent to evil ends. But in his jealousy and fear Iago reveals the mind of Mercury at its scheming best. His inner fire can only be used for his own advantage, or for revenge; he has no humanitarian motives, none that don't concern Iago. His wounded pride is so palpable that it has consumed its host, and almost become a character in its own right.

Shakespeare's other great Mercurial schemer is Cassius, whose 'lean and hungry look' depicts a side of Mercury that's so common it's become a cliche. These characters portray not only a narrow self-interest, but the antipathy that exists between Mercury and Mars, the two active, negative body types. Iago and Othello, Cassius and Caesar—Mercury and Mars. All have an instinctive distrust. They are like flint and steel, or oil and water; they just don't mix. At the opposite poles of activity, when these two negatively-charged types rub each other, their chemistries explode. You can find them at war in myth, in fantasy, in art and in literature, where the stealth of Mercury opposes the power of Mars.

Today's casting directors use this antipathy, and our instinctive reactions to it, in much the same way as the artists of the Renaissance used it to cast the models in their paintings. The cops in our movies are frequently Martial; honest, straight talkers who don't waste time being nice, and who achieve by their persistence what intuition, which they distrust, would arrive at in a leap.

Crooks and charmers are Mercurial; childish, shiny and too sharp to be honest. Tight shots show us their shifty eyes. This is the giveaway that lets us see through their disguise in a moment, and clues us as to who's the villain.

The ultimate in disguise comes from the combination of Venus and Mercury. Together these types can produce a chameleon who is compelled to obscure his own identity, one who has the ability to go unnoticed by others. The warmth of Venus can also temper the hard edges of Mercury, and give the quicksilver, changeable type a base in the earthy, sensuous world. But because the world of nature is—in its activity—amoral, Venus adds nothing positive to the sporadic, or opportune, morality of Mercury.

Sometimes a Difficult Life

The life I'm describing cannot be an easy one. Mercuries are besieged by energy that their bodies can't handle. They develop nervous tics and awkward mannerisms. They expect betrayal and, finding it everywhere, grow callous. They have trouble baring their emotional life, and think themselves shallow. Their occasional flare-ups surprise more moderate types. Role-playing eases their way in society, but also keeps an undercurrent of discomfort alive; they are alternately bemused and baffled by the effect their acting has on their audience.

Mercury is redeemed by its perception, wit and humor. The speed of their intellect gobbles facts and stores reams of scripts. They can be smooth talkers or inspired orators, hell-raisers or symbols for an aroused citizenry. We prize them for their bright air and their facile friendship. Mercuries amuse and entertain us as no other type can. They lift the clouds of our dullness and sweep us out of our doldrums. Even if it's only for a few minutes, we seem to fly into a finer air, and the electricity and brightness of their attention makes us, at those moments, giddy with life.

The Mercurial Type

General Orientation:
   Active-Masculine / Negative

Psychological Overview:
   Chief Features of power, manipulation, paranoia
   Maximum attraction of Jovial
   Maximum repulsion of Mars, the other active/negative type.

Key Words:
   'A little bundle of energy,' lively, opinionated,
   manipulative, deceitful, secretive, insecure, entertaining,
   bright, smooth-talking, honey-toned voice, 'lean and
   hungry'

Examples:

Richard Nixon	Sammy Davis, Jr.
Pierce Brosnan	Fred Astaire
Iago	

William Benham's Physical Description:
   In stature the Mercurial is small, averaging about five feet
six inches, compactly built, trim in appearance, tidy looking
and with a strong, forceful expression of countenance. His face
is oval in shape, features inclined to be regular, and the
expression changes rapidly, showing the quick play of his
mind. The skin is smooth, fine, and transparent, tending to be
olive in color, and shows the passing of the blood current
underneath, by easily turning alternately red or white when
excited, embarrassed, or in fear. The forehead is high and
bulging, the hair is chestnut or black and inclined to be curly
on the ends. The Mercurial grows a beard easily, which covers
the face well, and is generally a little darker than the hair, if it
be any color other than black. He likes to wear his beard
trimmed closely. The eyebrows are not thick but are regular
in outline, running to fine points at the ends, and sometimes

112

meeting over the nose. The latter growth is rare, however, belonging more distinctively to the Saturn. The eyes are dark or quite black, restless and sharp in expression. They look right at and seemingly through you, and sometimes produce the disagreeable but correct conviction that you are being estimated by one well able to do it. The nose is thin and straight, somewhat fleshy on the end; the lips are thin, evenly set and often a trifle pale or bluish in color. The whites of the eye frequently have a trace of yellow, as the Mercurial is of a nervous and slightly bilious type. His nervousness makes him breathe quickly and often through his mouth. The chin is long and sharp, sometimes turning up slightly at the end, completing the oval contour of his face. The neck is strong and muscular, connecting the head with shapely shoulders, lithe and sinewy and graceful in outline. The chest is large for the stature, well muscled and containing big lungs. The voice of the Mercurial is not full and loud, nor weak and thin, but is of medium timbre and possesses good 'carrying' quality. The limbs are graceful, giving him agility and the quickness of movement for which he is noted, as well as a power of endurance coming from muscular strength. His teeth are white, small in size and set evenly in the gums which are medium pink in color. Altogether the Mercurial impresses you as well knit, agile, and strong, not always beautiful, but shapely and well proportioned.

Mercurial Circulation

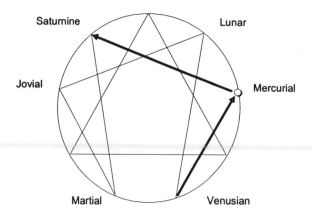

From Quickness to Stoicism

Although a masculine type, Mercuries don't completely lose the femininity they inherit from Venus, regardless of how slight it may seem to be. The vestiges of softness and body fat from Venus completely fall away. As the energy of the enneagram passes through Mercury, however, the masculinity entering here is developed more and more fully in the approach to Saturn.

This movement helps to add further definition to the Mercurial temperament. Mercuries can go a long way toward overcoming the somewhat scattered activity of their minds by acquiring some of the breadth or overview that Saturn has in abundance. And Mercury may find a cure for their cynicism about other people in the Saturn's even-handed fairness. Moreover, Mercuries can correct their own preoccupation with themselves by looking toward the ability of Saturn to address the needs of others.

Mercuries must be wary of the inhumanity that may arise from combining their own self-interest with the dominating plans of Saturn. It is by maintaining a focus on the humanity of the individual that they will be best able to harness the power of this transition, and by tempering their amorality with Saturnine restraint, can truly evolve toward a higher type.

Mercury-Saturn

This combination of types can be one of impatient dominance, cool and calculating, wrapped up in a vision of perfection, but still infected with the insecurities of Mercury.

Mercury-Saturn is almost always a well-built, attenuated body type, usually handsome and well defined. Combining quickness of intellect with breadth of vision, they may be drawn to writing, acting, or leadership roles. It is not a domestic type, unless well into Saturn, where paternal care will be more distinctly felt.

The unfortunate side of this combination joins facile Mercury to Saturn's organizational abilities, and may create a formidable criminal tendency. Easy in command but suspect of those around them, Mercury-Saturns may acquire leadership responsibilities but may not be comfortable for long in these parts. They will usually get along best with other Mercury-Saturns, lacking patience for slower or more naïve types. Their attraction is to Jovial-Lunar, their opposite, and may help to ground them in more humane values.

Examples:

Jeff Goldblum	Mercedes Ruehl
Christian Laettner	Frank Sesno
Daniel Day-Lewis	Cher

The Saturn Type

Moderation rules the Saturn world, and Saturns pay homage to it with restraint and self-denial. In this world spontaneity counts for little, unpredictability is a cardinal sin, and the righteous path is the one that seems safest. It is a world of cool, correct rationality, a world logically ordered and precisely planned.

Reflected in the facets of every Saturn's life is a sweeping, panoramic view. Their knowledge consists of a broad mix of facts, which they organize into a beautiful structure. Into this structure they fit new details as the need arises; they don't tamper with the edifice itself. Each fact bears weight, and each is treated equally. It's the orderly accumulation that Saturns admire, and which entrances them. The view this process yields of life tinges their relations with the other types, and gets ineradicably fixed.

Progress is an Important Value

Saturns approach each day as an opportunity to enhance some program that they've devised. Steady progress supplies the real joy they get from experiences, and gives them all the meaning they need. It leads them to arrange their lives in copious detail. They can start their list for the day with an instruction to themselves to 'wake up.' Why should any

119

moment be unaccounted for? An unplanned day looks to a Saturn the way a mine field looks to a soldier about to cross it; like chaos, where anything may happen, and he's compelled to prepare for it.

But he can accept help only on certain conditions. He would like you to remember the balance in his thinking. He would like you to realize that he will understand your information better than you do yourself, even while you're telling him where the mines are. He'll act the judge with you, and in a pose of judicial concentration will listen to your advice, nodding to himself as testimony proceeds. He's allowed you to say your piece, and will notify you later of his decision.

Hierarchy is the natural product of all this orderly thinking and the translation into the language of human interactions that comes most easily to Saturns. They want to know their place, and your place, in detail. They're interested in every measure of control and every line of authority that might affect them. Titles, credentials and qualifications give them a smooth method for classifying everyone, proofs of competence and approval that they can trust.

A Serious and Sedate Body Type

Saturns move seriously, behave seriously and play seriously. Their gravity adds force to their character and warns off the lighthearted. They aren't amused by your foolishness, but record it as judiciously as any other bit of information they come across. A Saturn is serious because he assumes life is serious; he can't see it any other way. Besides, without his gravity what good would all his regimens and disciplines be? At any moment decisions may have to be made, or an action may be called for. How will he know what's right? He'll have to consider closely...

Saturns are taller than most people, and tower over the other types. They find an advantage in their height; it's simpler to dominate someone who must look up to you. Saturns have an aristocratic air; their measured pace, thoughts of social elevation and scrupulous fairness assure them a place in society. They rise like cream in all sorts of organizations and find themselves managing companies, clubs or countries as chairmen, administrators or presidents.

It was some antique Saturn, I'm sure, who devised the art of delegation. This democratic way of work allows a department to excel if everyone does what he's been asked to do, assuming the overall strategy is sound. Of course, it's usually a Saturn who's doing the asking. He has the only copy of the complete plan, and you get the morsel he thinks you need to get your particular job done and no more.

The Comforts of Predictability

Predictable things comfort Saturns. I had a friend staying with me who confessed to this. He said his day could only start on a harmonious note if his breakfast were properly controlled. Each morning I'd find him at his meal, alone, with a plain white bowl he'd brought with him set squarely on the table. He was eating one of those cereals that righteously substitute nutrition for flavor, and which he had also brought along. His spoon lay perpendicular to him on the table, polished and packed for just this purpose. The importance he assigned to each tool was indicated by its position in the ritual. Needless to say, he also had some internal alarm that signalled the start of this monastic banquet—at the same moment each day.

Like Venusians, Saturns are at home with what seems safe. I've seen Saturns who, finding a restaurant they like in a new city, dine there every night for a week. Why aren't they drawn to variety like most of us? Their need for constancy is stronger, that's all. They'll sacrifice all the untasted novelties on the menu for the guaranteed pleasure of the prime rib they had last night.

For the same reason Saturns are insincere gamblers. Inching ahead on safe bets, they'll never shoot the works, or strive for that rush of abandon that lifts you when the odds get so steep you have to believe in magic to put your money down. They stick with their system instead, intent on the 'sure thing.'

They Can Deny Themselves

Here's a type that routinely denies itself. Saturns sometimes seem as though they are reason's revenge on humanity; their spontaneity has been drained, leaving them phlegmatic and a bit gray. They don't leap to opportunity, but carefully work out the pros and cons of every situation. They plan in order to avoid the pitfalls of life as much as to take advantage of its pleasures. A well-charted itinerary can make their hearts beat quick.

The Power of Facts

These people love the power of facts. A Saturn is sure that through facts he can prove his precision, his decisions and his rational muscle. He'll weigh all sides of a question and hope to come to some ultimate certainty. Nevertheless, he can just as easily lock himself in indecision when he gets the awful feeling that he might have to act before all the facts are in. So he'll spend hours mulling over what he knows, and rehearse the ramifications of all sorts of improbable events. But he's having a Saturnine kind of fun while he's at it.

It's no wonder Saturns like to count everything. They measure, judge and compare, generating data for further consideration. This is especially true for anything that can be calculated. Numbers seem ruthless to them, incontestable and free of messy uncertainty. Emotion, passion and unreasonable desires have no place in calculations, and are left out. This classifying ardor, putting everything in its proper place, inspires Saturns throughout their lives.

This is a 'Saturnine' Era

We're living in a *Saturnine* era—we think almost anything of value must be measurable, and anything we can measure must be of value. What's your IQ? How cold is it? Wind chill? Degree days? Rank of a tennis pro? Percent first serves, faults, unforced errors, record against under-21 year old left-handed players in rain on clay during June? New restaurant? Two stars, four forks and three dollar signs. Who's getting into Harvard this year? Combine the SAT's with the scores awarded for drive, connections and ambition and you'll know. Yes, it's everywhere.

With Saturn running wild, we're less sure of many things than we think we ought to be. Too many experiences don't answer to reason, and all our rationale hasn't made us more nimble when it comes to dealing with the unpredictable. At some point we learn the limitations of our own logic, and of the methods it's tried to impress on us. We look for new ways to understand, link them to our logical abilities and hope the combination creates a more powerful tool.

Saturns require a good deal of time to discover this and some never do. The dream of complete predictability never dies for them. Having confined their thoughts and plans within the rigid structures of hierarchy and priority, they get trapped there and can't find the way out. Form, rule and ritual assume the aspects of grace itself. Nebulous, messy or overly emotional experiences are replaced with a safe repetition of movements, meetings and sacraments that satisfy all their needs much more cleanly.

Enjoyment of Balance

Symmetry in design will please a Saturn, like the visual balancing you see in the works of the Flemish painter Jan van Eyck. These pictures always look to me like the result of a well-worked math problem. It's a type of display that pleases a Saturn exactly because it demonstrates its own internal order so forcefully. Stating the problem and showing its solution reinforce his commitment to structure and logic. He feels that to veer away from these principles will bring danger, with unpredictability looming in from every side.

Saturn is the type of regimentation and rule, law and legislation, and all the agreements we reach at various levels of society that allow us to live together. Their concern for equality and their literal interpretation of laws make Saturns great champions of the persecuted, including those who've been let down by these same systems. Many are avid and selfless workers for social justice. They are the Saturns whose reasoning about life happened to have grown into an idealistic, rather than a selfish, mold.

They Don't Need Many Pleasures

The mature Saturn at work is a wonder to behold. He goes from dawn to dusk no matter how dry or menial his task, and slakes his thirst with measured sips of water. It isn't as difficult for a Saturn to deny himself little pleasures this way as it would be for you or me. It's a conscious suppression of desires in favor of what his mind has told him is the most reasonable route to his eventual aim.

A Saturn seems more cut off from his own emotions and sensations than other people are. His heavy, serious face falls into a neutral expression when you're talking, as if deciding which response he's going to allow himself. This look also lets you know he's not enslaved by any of them. Saturns must be wired differently than other people. Maybe they have a switch that can be thrown to short-circuit the messages of pain or passion that would otherwise race from their minds— a neat trick that leaves them free to follow the plan of the day.

It's not surprising that a Saturn is most comfortable by himself, or with a fellow Saturn who can contribute independent teamwork, someone willing to work on a cooperative plan. In part, he isolates himself because he can't find anyone with the same standards of objectivity and decorum.

When he's with other people he's instructing them. He has advice to offer if you're buying tires or having a baby. Whether he owns a car or has a family himself doesn't matter. He's convinced he can think about your concerns better than you can, and he doesn't understand why you put so little value on his recommendations. Because he's protective, and because we fall so easily into error, this responsibility may be a burden, but it's one he can't ignore.

A Paternal Influence on Others

People thrive within Saturn's paternal atmosphere and in a circle of friends it's likely to be the Saturn who finds himself cast in the role of counselor, or confessor. Where Mercuries always look for the opportunity to act, and feel the stage constantly calling to them, Saturns wait for an opportunity to make subtle but important distinctions, and to point to a correct course of action. They want you to call on them to decide, to render an opinion, and when you petition a Saturn for guidance, he slips effortlessly into the role of the judge.

Nothing fits a Saturn's didactic nature so well as the prospect of being called on to arbitrate, to adjudicate, to distribute his wisdom and comprehension. This is his chance to educate you in the details of your own self-interest. He knows in every case what you should do, and what you shouldn't. If you're foolish enough to ignore his advice, he'll shake his head and wash his hands of the disaster you're about to bring on yourself.

He will wear the judge's robes he's donned whenever possible. He doesn't like to get involved in parochial fights, like the ones we have with a neighbor or competitor. Instead he waits for the chance to introduce his diplomacy, and is always available as a referee or a teacher. He wants you to make use of his sense of discernment. If he's allowed to rule unmolested, he'll always be on hand.

Father wields the rod at home, and Saturn is the authority in the house of types. But nothing is sacred in his schemes. He'll sacrifice what seem to be our most human drives in favor of the rules of a regimen he's invented. And once he gets going on one of his home-made programs, every part of his life can be called into question, analyzed and regimented.

For example, he'll program his sex life like a self-prescribing marriage counselor. Two nights a week, with a progress report on the third night. Saturns see nothing unusual about premeditation like this that might stifle others. But with Saturn, everything's a program. He eats an orange for the vitamin C; if it tastes good, that's a plus. Don't assume he's even noticed.

There's a mind like a sphinx in Saturns; their mental gaze seems permanently fixed on some far horizon. They leave us with the feeling that their ruminations are beyond our scope. The picture that we have of an absent-minded professor, bumbling in the details of life while his mind soars through abstract spheres, is one picture of Saturn.

Some Saturns are eccentric loners, absorbed in themselves, who go glassy when you mention the plumbing. Gaskets and joints have no place in their dreams of order and systematic action. Only the abstract, the theoretical and the planned are perfect enough to satisfy them. They get no bite out of life. It has none of the sting, none of the bittersweet pain that turns to pleasure, none of the blooming sensuality of life that exists only for itself, the way a hand moving over a lover's body exists only for itself.

They don't hit for the brute pleasure of contact, or gorge themselves, or pick a fight, or drink too much. On the other hand, you can't feel sorry for Saturns because the tempo and tone of their lives obviously please them so much.

They Have a Breadth of View

Saturns are drawn to philosophy and history, where their accumulation of facts has a noble tradition and their breadth of view has ample room to roam. We admire philosophy and history for just this reason, too, that they lift our own thoughts from the thicket of life and give us, for a moment, a more spacious view. It's a view that Saturns embrace and over which their minds sweep in a ceaseless search for patterns that can be made to conform to Saturnine principles of thought and action.

Looking over a corporation of which he is the head, a Saturn will try to find those large shifts of manpower and resources that will better organize or more efficiently produce the work of the company. He will try to find the generalities that are always true, the rules that guide the forces in events. From this he propounds a theory.

The broad view and the historical perspective make a Saturn moderate and discreet. Putting things in perspective separates him from more immediate feelings and he becomes aloof, detached. His concerns sweep over forces that move masses of people. These forces are so much larger than any individual that we sometimes wonder whether a Saturn can see those around him as friends, colleagues or lovers, and not just as impersonal *units*.

While a Saturn may be interested in humanity, he is just as capable of withdrawing from society. Saturns want to save you and guide you to truth because it's their mission, but with all this seriousness they don't come off well at parties. Their gravity points up our foolishness, suffuses us with a vague guilt and cools our wit. They remind us of the teachers, priests and parents whose voices still whisper inside us. They add weight to all our thoughts and pull from many people a long sigh of melancholy sobriety.

I suppose it's this leavening effect, and the limited repertoire of their expressions, that make us want to tease Saturns so much. We poke them, kid them and put them on in the hope of getting some kind of reaction, if we're confident enough to have overcome their reticence. We're challenged by the constancy of their demeanor, and want from them something more approachable than a cool judicious gaze.

Saturns are so serious that when we're in their company our choices of action are severely restricted. You can fall into their steady pace; you can fly into extreme and eccentric behavior out of frustration, or to change the tone; or you can leave. They are often in the same predicament. Without a group to dominate, a circle to educate, or a project to regulate, they're lost, and will soon find a corner in which they can patiently observe the oddities of humanity. Or they'll lose themselves in introspection. Perhaps they'll find another Saturn to share this moment with; at least another Saturn will understand.

Saturns Enjoy Other Saturns

Clumps of Saturns, like groves of trees, don't fidget or jump; the slow whisperings of their conversation are punctuated by equally slow pauses for reflection. They don't use their hands very much when they speak, marking only a crucial point here or there with a calculated gesture. Their height alone would set them apart, but combined with the formality of their movements and the equanimity of their mien, their height ensures that they'll always be noticed.

Saturns are just too decorous a type to be much fun. Too concerned with the right word, the best school, the appropriate remark. They're not going to sacrifice all their work for the sake of an impulse. And nothing is more unnerving than a Saturn, awkward and stiff, trying to be spontaneous because someone's told them to loosen up. You know instinctively they'll never succeed, and are grateful to see them restored to their propriety when the experiment's over.

A faculty for mental organization gives Saturns an intuitive grasp on how things are structured, how things work. From this sense springs their most constructive achievements. They can ignore their own desires to advance their plan, or the plan they've agreed to. It's his principles that compel a Saturn to carry each project to its completion.

His zest for structure and form may slip into dogma, and then he'll only be satisfied by strict rules and rigid procedures. His thinking gels in a fixed pattern, and the form of a ritual can acquire more meaning than what the ritual was designed to accomplish. Meetings are held because they've been scheduled, whether there is business to transact or not.

Moderation reigns and the mean becomes the road to salvation. Saturns set aims to an agenda. They carry them out with a deliberate, measured step, and track their progress on notebooks, calendars and checklists. We may not fathom what joy Saturns get from all this until we understand that for them the joy is in the doing—often in simply getting things done.

Can Be Too Dogmatic

Dogmatism of this sort can ruin a Saturn's efforts. The yearning for a great scope of understanding then crowds out the time it would take to penetrate any one subject in depth. The search for objectivity may cause him to lean heavily on formulas—an arrangement of ideas that will always be true.

He may start to demand that everything fit his way of thinking and discard the dynamic energy of contradiction. The tension that irreconcilable ideas give off can be cast aside in favor of neatness. The symmetrical solution must be the right one, no matter how synthetic. He gets mesmerized with order and may be tempted to seal off the chaotic sides of his own nature, the very wrinkles that could relieve his grayness and add a little color to his comprehension.

But Saturns do provide us with balance and care. At their best, the moderation, discipline and justice of Saturns come together to remind us of the nobility that lies in mortal men. The wisdom of Saturns speaks of some higher level of thought and action, that elevation of our highest potentials in which order, wrestled from the chaos of this world, is transformed into a divine harmony.

The Saturn Type

General Orientation:

    Active-Masculine / Positive

Psychological profile:

    Chief features of dominance or grayness

    Maximum attraction of Lunar

    Maximum repulsion of Jovial, with whom they compete for 'paternal' space in interactions.

Key Words:

    Gray, domineering, perfectionist, manipulative, intransigent, unable to reach decision, judicial, fair, hesitant

Examples:

George Bush	Sam Shephard
James Stewart	Vanessa Redgrave
Eleanor Roosevelt	Margaret Thatcher
Uncle Sam	Abraham Lincoln
Nolan Ryan	Al Gore

William Benham's Physical Description:

    The typical Saturn is the tallest of the seven types and his finger is the longest on the hand. He is gaunt, thin, and pale, his skin is yellow, rough, dry, and wrinkled, hanging in flabby folds, or else drawn tightly over the bones. His hair is thick and dark, often black, straight and harsh. His face is long, commonly called 'hatchet-shaped' from its thinness, his cheek bones are high and prominent, with the saffron-hued skin drawn tightly over them. The cheeks are sunken, with skin flabby and wrinkled. The eyebrows are thick and stiff, growing together over the nose and turning up at the outer ends. The eyes are deep set and extremely black, with a sad, subdued expression which changes only when flashes of anger, suspicion, or eagerness stir his mind. His nose is long, straight, and thin, coming to a sharp point at the end. The nostrils do not dilate as he breathes, but are rigid and stiff. His mouth is large, the lips thin and pale, the lower jaw and lower lip quite prominent and firm. If the Saturn has a beard it is dark, stiff, and straight, growing thickly on the chin and lip, but very sparse on the cheeks. The chin is prominent and large, the neck lean and long, with muscles showing prominently like cords, and the blue veins standing out under the shrunken and flabby skin. His Adam's apple is plainly in evidence. His chest is thin, the lungs seem cramped, as if operating in narrow, contracted quarters, and his voice as it comes through the thin lips is harsh and unpleasant.

The whole appearance of the Saturn impresses you with its lack of nourishment, lack of healthy blood supply, and its lean gawkiness; the dark, sad eyes, stiff, black hair, narrow chest, stooping shoulders, and shuffling gait all combine to bear this out. This is the typical Saturn. It is small wonder that, when the dashing Solars or Venusians, handsome, attractive, and magnetic, filled with the joy of living, meet him and try to fill him with their enthusiasm, the Saturn cannot feel their joy, or share their enthusiasm, but shakes his head mournfully, and thinks of how much sorrow there is in this world.

Saturn Circulation

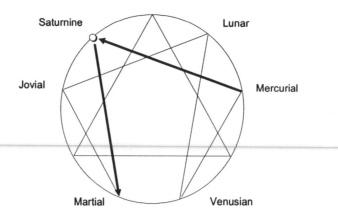

From Indecision to Action

Coming from Mercury, Saturn retains some of the hyper-kinetic energy of that type, but is toned down by the gravity inherent in Saturn. Passing through Saturn, restless activity wanes quickly and decisions may become more difficult and cerebral, as all possibilities need to be considered. The approach to Mars brings greater activity once again, albeit of a radically different kind.

In the move toward Mars, Saturns can counteract their indecision and 'paralysis by analysis.' They acquire the ability to get things done without losing the humane and judicial perspective so natural to Saturn. Mars lends them color and definition to combat their natural grayness, and provides the passion and commitment to a cause that they found lacking in their over-judicious nature.

However, if they simply inflate their somewhat eccentric ideas with the intensity of Mars, no good will result. But the progress that can be made toward self-actualization, in which the ideas of Saturn meet the energy of Mars, is truly great for this type.

Saturn-Mars

Saturn-Mars joins the physical and emotional activity of Mars to Saturn speculation, and the combination yields a thoughtful warrior, a passionate activist, or a committed revolutionary. This type is usually large, full-boned and with a well-defined musculature. Handsome and aggressive, the Saturn-Mars is well suited to business pursuits, is often found in active sports, and quickly takes on leadership in any group.

This is an ideal type whenever intelligent action is called for. Here Saturn finds a perfect complement, guiding the zealous Martial impulses. We know quite a bit about Saturn-Mars, considering that it epitomizes, and is the prototype for modern American cultural values. We see this in judicious use of force overseas and in aggressive social programs at home. The images we all maintain of active vitality, of goal-oriented living, of planning and actualizing aims in an orderly way, all owe something to this type.

In unfortunate examples, the Saturn-Mars may become violent or vicious, displaying both the Saturn's lack of concern for the individual as well as the Martial's willingness to cut through obstacles. And Saturn may well make some of the Martial's more extreme ideas seem reasonable. Whatever its field of activity, Saturn-Mars stands out.

Examples:

John Wayne	Marilyn Quayle
Prince Charles	Arnold Schwarzenegger
Queen Elizabeth I	Gary Hart
Burt Lancaster	Robert Redford

The Martial Type

Mars is an active, negative type whose influence moves through the enneagram at the final stage of the development of masculinity. The manliness that is so stoical in Saturn is intensified in Mars until it explodes in action, before fading on its way into Jovial.

Mars is violent, but it can be effective. It is energy in its purest and most indiscriminate form. In this type power comes to its fullest force; Martials hum with it. Energy floods the spirit of a Martial and overflows into everything he does. For a Martial, whether at the head of an army marching to war, or desperately wrestling with his inner demons, it's the energy of his actions on which he gets drunk.

A Martial's compact, powerful body and vivid, freckled complexion herald his arrival. Hair waving, his ruddy complexion flushed and a determined look in place, he strides right up to you and crashes through whatever conversation in which you may have been engaged. He thrusts his barrel chest out as far as his chin, and spreads his legs in a firm and ready stance.

Everything he's concerned with has an urgency and just won't wait. If you don't acknowledge him, or if you try to finish your conversation, the muscles in his neck bulge and perspiration covers his forehead as he tries to stare you into submission. If you don't give in to his bullying, he'll stomp off irate and disgusted, and mark you for a fool.

The Need for Goals

There's something in a Martial that won't let him live without a goal. Since he works from a plan, with specific points to be achieved, he finds a well-defined aim the most practical approach. Mostly, he trusts in what he can see. This goal-oriented approach seems as though simple concepts are all that are required to connect him with his team, his school or his country, and to give him a place to hang the pennants of his loyalty and fierce pride. He will work towards an aim in common with others if the work he's asked to do supplies him with visible, practical results. And he sticks to his job intently until it's done.

Martials don't know how to pass an aimless life, or even an aimless day. To those of us who are more passive, or more changeable, who enjoy an unplanned ramble through a new city, or who can shrug off the tour we've scheduled in favor of a few magical hours loitering in a street-side cafe—to all of us, Martials look obsessed.

A Martial can become a man unable to live without something to do, something to be working on, tyrannized by his own ceaseless drives. His aims and plans can squeeze him into a life of measured progress and undeflected, joyless striving. Or they can send him thrusting and crashing through his days, pursuing one credential or achievement after another.

A Military Influence

Ferocity, loyalty and vitality, the hallmarks of the consummate military man, also help to define this body type.

Martials' minds and bodies snap naturally into military postures, which accounts for their disciplined attitudes. It's a posture, a way of approaching life, that seeps into their thinking, eating, sleeping, dressing, driving, talking, loving and dying.

They have the wariness of the professional soldier at the front, and his feisty abandon at play. Martial men like to go carousing, and drink themselves into a stupor. Martial women grow out of their 'tomboy' childhood, and go on to become athletic and competitive achievers, pioneering new roles for women.

Going on vacation with a Martial may make you think you're on a military campaign. He knows intuitively that surprise will be of decisive advantage in his plan of battle. Lightning attacks on museums and other temples of culture reveal the strategy that propels him in this cause.

He manages to take yards of paintings hostage, captures acres of sculpture with a quick look. His pace never flags. Are there eight sights on the day's itinerary? The order of battle is drawn. Maximum use of transport, supplies and resources is thoroughly planned. Precise allowance is made for efficient utilization of time at each target site. It's a bit of astute planning he thoroughly enjoys.

Hotel is base camp where maps and guides are assembled. The real fun of logistics, timing and fall-back positions comes next, because Martials are very realistic about all the things that can go wrong and foul their plans. Step by step the Martial proceeds, and each completed segment of the day is a victory. He gets his joy from checking off the stages of his progress, from the visible confirmation that he's done what he set out to do.

Loyalty is an Important Value

This regimented world is infused with the air of latent power. Martials are warriors, and the logic of the battlefield never completely leaves them. A Martial relies on his friends the way a soldier in his foxhole relies on his buddies, but he may require that you prove your affection or demonstrate your loyalty before you convince him of your sincerity.

The first thing a Martial wants to know about you is simple; are you a friend or a foe? If you tell him you're neutral, he thinks it's a trick, that you're feinting, or that you're hiding your true feelings. He can admit that he's not sure of some people's loyalties, but it's a strain on his ethics. He can't be comfortable with people who won't take a stand, and he won't know how to act with you until he finds out onto which side of the fence you're going to fall.

Above all, Martials value direct and simple talk, which they understand as easily as they do direct and simple action. They rely on people to mean what they say, and are impressed by a blunt truth no matter how painful it is for them to hear it. Martials expend their energy on the crises which litter their lives, and which make everything troublesome and wearying. The intensity it takes to keep putting out fires gives them the added pleasure of an excuse to subordinate their own interests and comforts in order to deal with the prevailing emergency.

Admired for their Vitality

If we admire Saturns for their counsel, and Venusians for their warmth, we admire Martials for their vitality. When you need something done, it's a Martial that you want to have on call. He can slash red tape, fire a stalled project and plow through maddening detail. He'll rake your yard, re-do your den and hang your pictures—faster than you can. He knows the perfect time to do whatever needs to be done: *now*. These people are designed for action. They get their results not because they can do so much, but because they never stop until the job's done.

Brimming with intensity, a Martial burns his volatile fuel driving through activities, and when he gets keyed up, he's fierce. Once he's touched by something he accelerates quickly through his emotions, and soon arrives at a peak of agitation. Whether he's revelling at his local pub, or beginning to steam at some politician, he comes to a head in a minute, and stays there until his energy is spent.

For a Martial, infatuation can turn to obsession in an instant. Then he dashes into an affair, becomes the ardent lover and may spontaneously fly halfway around the world in hot pursuit of the latest object of his desires. The scent of conquest dizzies him; his focus narrows, he won't swerve from his hunt, he never listens to reason and he may well become unstoppable.

Drawn to Extremes

Martials live in extremes, and are drawn to the rough edges of life, where everything seems more exciting. They can be civil and well-behaved at the office, but when there's no hint of danger or controversy, they feel only half-alive. Their restlessness is constant. It doesn't leave them whether they're mowing the lawn or wrestling a sculpture from stone. There's a force behind their actions, and a heat that burns through obstacles.

Martials don't mind finding themselves in a tight corner; it justifies the ruthlessness that will be necessary to get out of it. And although they're usually open about their plans, don't think they're always being honest, or that they're incapable of a strategic deception once in a while. Their strength lies in the unspoken commitment they've made to themselves: to overcome whatever is blocking their way. It gives them a reason to exploit all of their resources, to hold nothing back. And this in turn is really a challenge to themselves: "Can I overcome this obstacle, and prove myself worthy?" Perhaps it is the necessity they feel to continually find this proof of their own self-worth in defying the odds and denying themselves that jump starts the incredible 'motor' of a Martial.

Firebrands and Revolutionaries

Martials regularly appear in the front ranks of protest marches, hunger strikes and political rebellions. They chafe at negotiations and would rather test their power face to face against their opponents. They are the firebrands and revolutionaries, inflamed and loyal to a cause, who are out to stir up the populace. They seem doomed to be always in opposition, and their rebellious nature eventually gets them in trouble. After the fight's been fought and won, they don't see the need to modify their extreme rhetoric or their rebellious pugnacity, and soon find themselves on the outside again, smoothly replaced by more manageable types.

Martials are impatient with long-term settlements, won't stand any nick in their principles, and think that social change will soothe the itch they've got. They seem naïve to someone less literal, as if they were unprepared to deal with people who know how to hide their motives.

Most of our views of Martials show them restless and in motion. It's rare to find one in repose because when he's not absorbed in work, he's working out. You'll see him jogging in the morning, pacing in his office and squirming at the opera. He always seems to be on the move, dashing across town or trekking in Tibet. He's comfortable outdoors, where his pioneer spirit and his thirst for freedom of action can run unchecked.

A Fiercely Independent Type

One source of a Martial's pride is his self-reliance. He considers himself the best choice for most projects, and doesn't see how anyone else could possibly do as good a job. He would rather build his house himself, without anyone else to slow him down. If you offer to help, he'll probably refuse because he sees you as an obstacle, and wants to be left to work at his own frenzied pace.

He insists on his independence, and values others who seem as self-sufficient as he. A Martial thinks people who surround themselves with friends, or who find plenty of acquaintances with whom they can chat away the hours, are weak. But he gets frustrated with himself when his bluntness—or his barroom humor—drives others away.

Small talk unsettles Martials. Banter bores him unless it's got an edge, or shows signs of escalating into an argument. He loves to find a flaw in your reasoning, and hopes you'll take his attack as the chance for a brawl. Then he really comes alive. Zeroing in on you like a pilot screaming down on a bombing run, he finds the crack in your defenses and drops his load. He'll rarely miss an opportunity to attack, and expects you to fight back. But if you try attacking him first, he takes your criticism too hard, and sulks away convinced he's been treated unfairly.

Looking for Mars

If you're looking for Mars, look for the frontal assault, the provocative remark, the direct opposition. Behind them you'll find a Martial, itching for a fight. He's blunt, and tries to shock you. He'll adopt a rigid moral stand, or a purposefully crude tone to get your attention, or to get you mad; it's the same to him. He gets a thrill from opposing you no matter what you've said, and hammers away just to test your fortitude.

When he's riled, you can't deal with a Martial. If you say he's being unreasonable, that everything is ambiguous and life is full of contradictions, he presumes you're feeble. He's taken a stand on principle, and won't be budged. He demands that you take a stand too, and goads you with his brutal logic and insinuations of weakness until you either stand up and fight or walk away.

Oddly enough, he doesn't want to convert you to his position, because then he'll always distrust your commitment. Martials want loyalty from us, or they don't want us at all: *America, love it or leave it! My country, right or wrong!* Although he may think your ideas are mistaken, nothing will rouse his scorn so much as your deserting those same ideas.

A Martial swings his spade at intruding weeds in the garden with the same resolute violence which, in another age, he used to swing his awful sword at rows of his enemies. He knows only one way to do things: with vigor. Compromise is a sin to him, and diplomacy the habit of lying about your own feelings. He has little use for subtleties, which leave him frustrated. The explanations he appreciates are short and to the point.

An Example of Mars

I used to live with a Martial who always gave me the impression that she was engaged on a great commission, no matter how ordinary her errand turned out to be. Her boot steps echoed throughout our house, beating a cadence of resolve and determination, even if she was only collecting the mail. I could tell what room she was in, and in what direction she was headed, and never feared that I wouldn't know when she'd arrived home or was going out. The vigor with which this woman washed dishes—the bang of the pots, the slam of the doors—echoed the vigor of her walk.

Martials are no good for stealth or covert manipulations. They would always rather tell you what they think and take the consequences. Their distrust of Mercuries seems primal, and if they find themselves in the same room with one, every muscle in their body can bristle with irritation.

Martials and Venusians

A Venusian, however, is the ideal mate for a Martial. In a Venusian's lush passivity he finds a home for all his raging potency, no matter how rough it becomes. His energy thrills and enlivens a Venusian, who in turn evokes the Martial's more intimate feelings by appeals to his rough sensuality and protectiveness.

As long as a Martial isn't put off by Venus' apathy and passivity, this connection of types creates relationships, marriages and affairs of great passion. Martials can be gentle with their children, but they also mix rigorous discipline and harsh expectations into their education.

Sexual Vigor

Sexual vigor runs through Mars as potently as physical vigor does, and the type glows with it. Sex is one of the constants in the programs Martials have devised to reduce tension; they have an instinctive sense that sexual frustration can make them explode. They need sexual release more than anyone else, and without it may sink into an unfriendly funk. The sexuality in Martials, combined with their physical vigor and their explosive temper, produces a nature more inclined toward violence than any other type. They simply have too much energy for the demands that life puts on them.

Although this is the same energy that fuels their ambition and drive, it also punishes their bodies. You'll notice a Martial grinding his teeth, bulging his neck and tensing his back so habitually that if you try to give him a massage, his body feels like wood or steel, not flesh and blood.

High on the Scent of Danger

With all this tension and energy surging through them, it's not surprising that Martials overdo things a bit. A Martial goes at life like one of those practitioners of karate—a *martial* art—who takes our breath away simply by trying to break taller, more unlikely stacks of bricks each time he swings. Martials get high on the scent of danger, and feed their addiction by driving too fast, hanging out of tall windows, or learning sky diving—where they get the additional thrill of throwing themselves from an airplane.

You see Martials in California's Yosemite Valley, where they hang suspended a few thousand feet up a sheer granite wall. They are the ones riding dog sleds in the arctic wilds, enthusiasts and explorers, brutally overcoming one barrier after another. The concentration required for these feats turns them into juggernauts, and reminds me of the early Christian crusaders who marched for thousands of miles across countries filled with hostile forces, their eyes fixed on Jerusalem.

Martials are out setting records while you and I are at the office. They're pioneering new territories, making the necessary sacrifice. They throw their comforts away like chains that had tied them down; now they can get something done. They play at games and sports when hurt, determined not to baby themselves. They're certain they can always force their bodies farther, disregard their doctors' advice, think medication is for the weak, and, having gone beyond their endurance, make their bodies pay the price.

Even at a cocktail party, watch a Martial on the terrace where, like everyone else, he's leaning against a railing. But the Martial's compelled to lean just a little farther out over the edge, thrilling himself with the rush that fear brings. He's heady on the lunatic brew that's boiling inside him. While one voice in his head is telling him to stop, another is urging him to jump; the adrenaline produced by this internal tug-of-war is one of a Martial's favorite feelings. It gives him something to struggle against when life threatens to become boring.

This struggle is what a Martial is after; he's honing his resolve against it. Difficulties are his insurance that he won't go soft. When he is uncertain about the solution he's found to a problem at work, or the course his team should take, he bullies his fears and bashes his doubts, and just charges ahead.

To succeed in this world, he thinks, is to rule by your own force and iron self-discipline.

In the Business World

Martials may be impatient with civility and routine, but they quickly grasp the attractions of modern business life. Here they find a strict hierarchy, with its comforting and concrete labels and rewards. They feel that if they locate the paths of power and spar nimbly enough, they'll have an objective measure of their success: dollars and cents. Martials flourish in sales, where the intoxication of the hunt unleashes the full force of their competitive drive.

Mars in the Arts

Of course, they're not all mercenaries and pugilists, and many Martials have taken their considerable zeal into less bloody arts. The paintings of Vincent Van Gogh, for instance, illuminate the type, stunning us as they do with their unconventional and perceptive vitality. Forms roil across Van Gogh's canvases, where he's traded delicacy for a demonic intensity. We can feel him caught in the grip of a great urgency, almost too piercing to bear. Yet he's channeled the violent energy of Mars within his own vision.

Ludwig van Beethoven, who outraged his contemporaries with his lusty and revolutionary music, demonstrates another side of Martial. He played the piano with an intensity that made the instrument jerk across the salon floor, and achieved heights of musical invention and dramatic effect despite the obstacles that dogged his days.

Martials are a pugnacious and feisty bunch, but I see their shortcomings most clearly in their need for difficulties. Hardships vivify them. Their insatiable drive gives them little leisure, but alerts them to potential disasters everywhere. They can't stop worrying about the blemishes in their lives, and only want a chance to wrestle one-on-one with the demons they find there. They're sure that problems are coming around every corner every day, and get themselves so geared up for battle that they can't go through a supermarket, or wash the car, without throwing off at least a hint of frenzy.

It's remarkable, in a way, that the native skepticism of Mars doesn't poison their drive more than it does. Although a Martial can sink into a gloomy and rancorous depression, it's only a new challenge he's waiting for. When the resistance of a difficult project, a tough game, or an unexpected setback appears he puts away his misgivings and his fears, buffs up his persistent energy, and sets off to reach the goal on which his determined eyes have happened to alight.

The Martial Type

General Orientation:
> Active-Masculine / Negative

Psychological Overview:
> *Chief features* of aggression and destructiveness
> *Maximum attraction* of Venus
> *Maximum repulsion* of Mercury

Key Words:
> Angry, rash, unpredictable, destructive, aggressive, determined, critical, violent, dedicated, warrior, passionate, impulsive, loyal

Examples:

James Cagney	Sean Penn
John F. Kennedy	Katharine Hepburn
Vincent Van Gogh	Paul Newman
Richard Burton	Nick Nolte
Sissy Spacek	Ross Perot

William Benham's Physical Description:

The Martial is of medium height, very strongly built, muscular looking, carries himself erect, shoulders back, and has the appearance of one ever ready to defend himself. His head is small, bullet shaped, with an unusually large development at the base of the brain. The back of the neck is broad and, in a pronounced specimen, developed much above the average. The face is round, the skin thick and strong, red in color, and often presenting a mottled appearance. The hair is short, stiff, sometimes curly and of an auburn or red color. The beard is short and harsh. The eyes are large and bold looking, with a bright expression, dark in color, and with the whites often bloodshot, showing the great strength of his blood supply. The mouth is large and firm, the lips thin with the under one slightly the thicker. The teeth are small, regular, strong, and yellowish in color. The brows grow thick, straight, and low over the eyes, giving often the appearance of a scowl. The nose is long, straight, or of the Roman type, the chin firm and strong, often turning up slightly at the end. The ears are small, and set close to the head, the red color of skin being quite prominent around them, this red often turning to a purple, congested appearance with strongly marked subjects. The neck is short and thick, connecting the head with a finely developed pair of shoulders, broad and muscular, with large muscles running down the back and a big expansive chest. In this chest is a pair of large, strong lungs which send forth a big commanding voice full of resonance and power. The legs are short but stout and muscular, the bones of the body are big and strong, the feet are broad and the instep inclined to be flat, making the subject walk in a proud, determined manner. Altogether he shows himself one well able to force his way through the world, mentally if he can, physically if he must. The Martial by his very appearance shows his true character, full of fight, either aggressively or in self-defense, mentally or physically, a strong, robust constitution, and one ardent in all things.

Martial Circulation

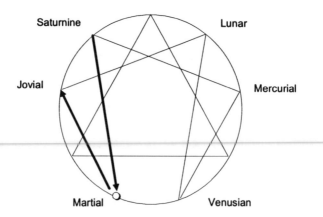

From Action to Concern

Arriving from Saturn, Mars is in the full flood of activity and masculinity. Unhampered by the brooding, judicial impulses it has thrown off, Mars at its height has almost no reins on the free expression of its passions. As it moves toward Jovial it will be softened and deepened, while retaining its intensity.

In the move toward Jovial, Martials can correct the rashness of some of their actions by acquiring a measure of concern for others. They may stop to consider the consequences of their actions on others. Where Mars may have made them destructive in the desire for action, Jovial can temper this ruthlessness and inability to control their enthusiasms. And while Mars delights in the presence of danger, mindless of its effect on others, Jovial will bring a depth of feeling that can turn this tendency to more positive uses.

Martial

Martials must avoid adding Jovial depth to their most violent feelings, which is not progress at all. They need to watch for the maudlin impulses of Jovial taking hold of their virulent feelings, resulting in a demonic and possibly vicious character.

Mars-Jovial

In the Mars-Jovial combination, passion is allied to humanistic aims, although the Martial intensity may simply be supercharged by Jovial depth of feeling. Mars adds an element of activity to the Jovial that other passive types lack, and the Mars-Jovial type cannot be considered a passive type at all. The journey through Jovial eliminates most masculine elements, adding depth but subtracting activity and raw energy.

This type will often have the ruddy coloring of the Martial married to the overstuffed look of Jovial. As an aggressive people-pleaser with the ability to get things done, Mars-Jovial is perhaps the most accomplished type in business. They are frequently found at the head of corporations, in the diplomatic world, as salespeople or running their own business. The type may have a predilection for alcoholism, for wild over-spending or other indulgent behavior.

The Mars-Jovial can be seen as passion in action or depth with brashness, but it can also become sentimental and self-defeating when focusing its prodigious emotions on feelings of self-deprecation and defeat.

Mars-Jovial, like Venus-Mercury, straddles the active/passive line, providing it with even more inner contradictions than normal. Here the struggle is between the warrior, always ready to rise to a fight, and the forgiving king, anxious to make peace. These strong forces must be reconciled for the individual to come to terms with themselves, and for inner harmony to grow.

Examples:

Bette Midler	Teddy Roosevelt
Barbara Bush	George Gurdjieff
Pablo Picasso	Spencer Tracy
Janis Joplin	

The Jovial Type

The Jovial is a strangely active type. After all, this is the first of the three passive types, but Jovials don't stay isolated from other people, like Lunars, or vegetate like Venusians. Perhaps it's a residue of the intense activity of Mars that seeps into the type. This would account for the intensity with which they fling themselves into projects, and the energy with which they pursue deep understanding.

When you see how a Jovial gets flushed with his latest enthusiasm, how he immerses himself in his subject, how he yearns to know every fact and name connected with it, how he airs his discoveries to all his friends and how he draws many of these friends into his excitement, it's hard to recall that Jovial is a passive type.

But in Jovial this is an on-again, off-again enthusiasm. They may be excited today about their latest cause, but that doesn't mean that next week they won't be on a new diet, in a new sport or studying art instead of selling stock.

Unable to resist the new, Jovials live a life of flux. They smell in novelty the giddy aroma of change, and succumb to it again and again. They get no solace from routine; it's routine that makes them itchy to move, that makes them long to ride the swell of something entirely new.

Cycling from peaks of enthusiasm through valleys of boredom, Jovials may accomplish little. They don't penetrate far enough, don't last through the rough spots that only discipline and persistence might help them with, soon their interest begins to fade, their enthusiasm drains away and eventually all their energy for their subject has departed.

A Colorful Type

This is a colorful type, even outrageous. At its extreme, a Santa Claus type, but usually with round faces, round cheeks and round shoulders, to go with their rounded outlook on life. Jovial men are more feminine when they're near Lunar, but Mars firms and intensifies them. Their hair falls out faster than their paunch expands, but not too much faster. The concert hall audiences and the musicians playing for them both contain a high percentage of glittery Jovial heads; maybe it's the creativity inherent in their type.

Jovials like to make a splash in society, and use all their theatrical ploys to get themselves noticed. They heighten their dramatic entrances by the extravagance and range of their wardrobes. Their closets are stuffed with clothes which will become the costumes for the many roles a Jovial has to play. They're likely to have a variety of sizes on hand as well, confident that their fleshy bodies will continue to rhythmically expand and contract.

A Jovial's sweeping exits are just as impressive. He flings kisses and calls in all directions, throws his coat around his ample body, and all in all uses the drama and volume of his departure to leave the most vivid impression behind. He's always on stage.

Rembrandt - An Exemplar of Jovial

The Dutch painter Rembrandt van Rijn was a fully-fledged Jovial, who painted himself and his models in the most fantastic and exotic costumes. This translation of his Joviality into his art is natural, and doesn't surprise us. Even a Dutch fishmonger in one of his paintings, weighted down by the opulent robes of some Turkish potentate, doesn't make us flinch.

Many novelties crossed Rembrandt's path. He lived in Amsterdam, the hub of a trading empire where all the fruits of trader nations were brought by the sailors and merchants amongst the seventeenth-century Dutch. He had so little resistance to these strange treasures that he eventually bankrupted himself and left the auctioneers costumes, gold helmets, Japanese armor and antique busts with which to pay his many creditors.

Yes, Jovial is a prodigal type, wasteful and extravagant with money, lavish and reckless with promises. They provide so much entertainment for others, and so much succor, that we can't find it in us to hold their self-indulgence against them. A Jovial's parties attract just as many people when he's down and out as they do when he's thriving. He'll still feed you too much, make you laugh with his stories, and soothe your problems. Poverty doesn't force him to pull in the wings of his flamboyance; he lets it soar on credit instead.

A 'Bright' Attraction

This is a maternal type, fussy and caring. Its influence sometimes alternates with that of Saturn—a paternal type—and sometimes opposes it. Jovial finds a complement in childish and entertaining Mercury, and the attraction between these two is bright and electric. Together their wit

165

flashes quick and keen, with a sharp and ready edge. They may also collapse into fits of bubbling hysteria that contort them both, and whoever else happens into their company, in spasms of laughter.

Mercury is really the perfect foil for Jovial. A Mercury's quick mind can keep up with a Jovial's circuitous reasoning, and Mercuries' hypochondria allows Jovials to indulge their need to nurture and care for others. Mercuries hunger for attention as voraciously as children do—a hunger that complements Jovials' need for students to lecture, to guide and to counsel.

Like Mercuries, Jovials thrive in society. A Jovial loves to have people around, and as long as there isn't another Jovial to contend with, the more people there are the better he'll like it.

People are the medium he lives in, the air he breathes. His address book bulges with the names of friends, associates and acquaintances. He'll have the number of a stranger he struck up a conversation with on a train to London twelve years ago: But what an interesting person! If he happens to come across this name, he sets off on the tale—he thinks each of his stories is equally fascinating. Once launched, he doesn't need more than your nod to keep him going.

How Jovials See Themselves

Jovials would like you to think that they only see the best in the people around them, but their gossip has a catty tone. They're committed to maintaining the bright and cheerful image they've got of themselves, and won't give up the stubborn optimism that makes it work. It's difficult to get helpful criticism from a Jovial, even when you want it. To criticize you pains him; either he's reluctant to hurt you with the truth, or afraid that he'll sacrifice his popularity by telling you something you didn't want to hear.

The fragility of a Jovial's self-esteem causes him to talk about other people in the rosiest terms. He's horrified by what might happen if he's honest and plain. He'll be affronted if you disagree with him, but he'll be mortified if you hint that you don't like him. Vanity makes him vulnerable to the manipulations of flattery and the humiliations of defeat. He thinks he's never wrong, or unlikable; according to all his evidence, Jovial is the *perfect* type.

The Flaw of Vanity

This vanity can turn all his diamonds to dust. His easy prominence in social situations, the way he attracts people into his sphere of influence, everything that makes a Jovial popular, entertaining or respected can turn against him. His vanity turns his humor into an ornament of his character. And while he can spot his friend's defects or his wife's obsessions as well as anyone can, his own conduct seems wonderful to him, his aims have true nobility, and his behavior borders on the sublime. He's likely to think: "I must certainly be a fine and entertaining fellow. Why else would all these nice people like me?"

Vanity pumps up a Jovial with ostentation, self-interest and pomposity. Vanity inflates him with nervous confidence, behind which hides a delicate bubble of fear, a secret so fragile that it must be protected from the pinpricks of his own doubt. He refuses to accept the help offered by his friends, and thinks that loyalty means you'll never criticize him.

This folly distorts many of the talents of a Jovial. While he harmonizes the chords struck by each person around him into a fruitful and cooperative tune, it takes only one person who refuses to follow his score to drive him wild. He weaves insightful and amusing stories for an audience, but smothers any scent of competition under smoke clouds of pointless verbosity, and ends up becoming a bore.

A Jovial may be a natural teacher, but he's the one you can't disagree with. He champions underdogs as long as they show their gratitude. He is an untiring organizer, insists on his firm sense of right and wrong—but he also wants to be sure you've spelled his name right on the program credits.

Yet by these devices a Jovial's vanity is thwarted and fails to reach its own goal. A Jovial feels that his faults blot his perfection, that his errors will drive people away. He may become pompous and evasive. But his friends wish he'd see his excesses the way they do, as pointing up his humanity, for which they would love him.

Jovial Appetites

Jovials enjoy being teased and titillated; it revs their engine. They're after the spice in life, and want to take in everything. Their appetites are pricked by curiosity, including their appetite for the new, the strange and the odd. They collect stories about enigmatic characters, mementos of dramatic moments from their past, eccentric fragments of life. Their shelves overflow with the stuff and they won't part with a penny of it; the chaos that results is a reminder of their travels, the wide range of their interests, how complex and multifaceted they must be. They live amidst a clutter of collectibles and are comforted by them.

A Jovial is a kind and forgiving friend who welcomes you into his family. He'll loan you his car, find you a job, cook dinner for you, and slip you some cash to tide you over. He's ready to accept the responsibility for your happiness and well-being. He's distressed by the suffering of his friends or his family, or anyone else touched by his expansive feelings. He would like to help you through your times of difficulty and is willing to help you carry your burden as if it were his own.

It's hard for Jovials to fathom the utter randomness of disease and pain; the injustice of it defeats them. Their world, although colorful and varied, has more happy endings than ours does. Regardless of how low you've fallen, how desperate your circumstances look or how dim your prospects seem to be, a Jovial will manage to find a silver lining to the cloud hanging over you. To pragmatic people— or those more cynical or ironic—Jovials simply seem unrealistic, the kind of people destined to be disappointed because they've never noticed that, in life, disasters are routine.

A Jovial remains a determined optimist about himself and his friends. He'll support your ambitions wholeheartedly as long as you treat his advice with the gravity it deserves. If you wonder how to get his backing, try to determine the role into which he's cast himself. He may have decided to be your counselor, your teacher, your mother or your guru. You run a risk if you step outside the role of the moment, and you may bring down on yourself the cruellest punishment that a Jovial can inflict on you—exile. He can't imagine anything more terrible than depriving you of his company.

This threat of exile is the sword a Jovial holds over your head, his punishment for bad behavior. Please him and all his caring attention is yours; disappoint him, and he'll cut you off completely, as if you'd never existed. His preoccupations are all variations on a theme of debt and obligation. He lures you with promises of favor and corrects you by playing on your guilt.

Passive Power

Jovials seem to have a direct line to our fear of doing the wrong thing, which they systematically play on to keep us in line. If you can't step back from your desire to please people you may find yourself cast as a satellite to their star, and find it painful to disconnect from their influence.

A Jovial's power depends on his ability to arouse you, to move you, to make his vision seem like your vision. The sweep of his thinking and his flair for the dramatic enable him to convince you, if only for a moment, that parking his car, or stopping at the store, or whatever errand he's sent you on is one step in the march of human progress, and an honor he rarely bestows.

We're screened from the motives that may be driving a Jovial by the bluff and bluster that obscure his actions. Even his tact can get caught up in his manipulations. And it may never occur to us, when we're involved in his call for selfless service, that a Jovial's purpose may have a darker side which is just as hidden from him. He's become drunk on his own righteousness, and doesn't mind a little veiled seduction to get his way.

Jovials enjoy their capacity for pure power, the ease with which they control other people. They'll coerce co-workers or manipulate circumstances to earn an advantage. Aroused by a threat to their family or their prestige, they're ruthless.

But Jovials also get caught by the demands of their well-defined self-portrait, in which they've painted an idealistic and utopian shape to their ambitions. They become experts at strategic omissions and develop into elegant justifiers. They use all the art they can muster not simply to explain to you what they've done and why, but to reassure themselves at the same time.

An instinct for tact leads Jovials to success in diplomatic posts. Their commitment to harmony anchors their dedication to family, community or country, in all of which they seek cohesion and balance. They may find themselves bringing opposing parties to a negotiating table, or arbitrating between warring friends. What they dispense is approval and support, not justice.

Rhetorical skills and personal magnetism launch Jovials into political life. They're well-suited to both trade and business, and may be chosen to run a company after they've demonstrated their competence and responsibility.

The Jovial Atmosphere

Being near a Jovial has a tonic effect on other people, and inspires their trust. The most reassuring and sympathetic doctors we meet are Jovials; somehow they not only share our pain, but make us feel they've helped our cure with a touch or a smile. They are the rare and sympathetic healers who are never too tired to stop by to see you, who always seem to have sweets in their pocket for any children they may come across.

Jovials have enough energy to support a small village of dependents, and surround themselves with cats, dogs, children, friends, family and colleagues. They love languages and learn them readily. Their acting translates effortlessly to the stage, where they can satisfy their craving for extreme behavior while getting high on the prospect of fame.

Jovials like to spend money whether they have it or not; nothing will raise their spirits as fast as a little foray into conspicuous indulgence. They are neither humble about their talents nor discreet about their assets. They tickle themselves with the daring of their excesses; if you don't notice their diamond earrings, their alligator boots or their new Chevrolet, what good are they? An abundance of cash gives Jovials a satisfied, well-fed look, as if they had earned the reward of self-indulgence.

The Creative Thread

A creative thread runs through some of this behavior. It glimmers in Jovials' constant re-imagining of themselves, the ongoing thrill of being on stage, the challenge of pure performance. It surfaces in their wit and in the way their humor points out the contradictions and absurdities of life, yet leaves us gasping and holding our sides.

From Jovial farm girls aquiver with the synthetic lyrics of popular songs, to Jovial industrialists stirred by their collections of corporate art, even to the booming Jovial voice of Walt Whitman celebrating himself and the universe, people of this type find art and crowd it into their lives.

Both the life of a musician, and music as a rest from life charm them equally. As parents and artists they are prolific. Johann Sebastian Bach, a Jovial who produced music all his life as easily as most of us breathe, fathered more than thirty little Bachs as well.

The history of art certainly isn't a strictly Jovial domain; it's much too human and too varied a pursuit, and one that has a place for every type. But crowding all around you'll find Jovials trying to satisfy the craving they've got for art in any form.

They become patrons of artists, art historians, curators, symphony supporters, opera fund-raisers, endowers of new museum wings and friends of conductors. I'm not sure I've ever met a Jovial who didn't either write poetry, or read it. Without much perseverance a Jovial flits from one experiment to another, makes a film one year, throws some pots the next and always seems on the verge of signing up for yet another evening course that's struck his fickle fancy.

But all this art and eclecticism tells us something else about Jovials, something that's also reflected in the cohesiveness they work on others. It tells us about a longing bred into them, that spreads through much of their thought and behavior; a longing for harmony.

When I say harmony, however, I mean that Jovials cast themselves as the harmonizing force. Mere order won't satisfy them, the kind that discipline gives you, or the order that flows from a strict sense of form. They're after something different—connections in meaning, not chronology.

Jovials want to understand everything in depth, they want to connect every fleeting feeling, every new thought and every second of experience to every other feeling, thought and experience. They may have a map of the meaning of life, but it doesn't satisfy them. They want to strip it from the wall and wrap it around a globe, get an idea of the real relationships at work between things.

When they try to extract meaning from the tiniest scraps of experience Jovials can sound absurd about as often as they seem profound. The distinction is one that matters little to a Jovial who's on a roll, audience in hand, casting his mind over wider and wider tracts of time in the search for connections, correspondences, explanations and coincidences.

Some people think that this habit, which contributes so much to the part they play in society, is propelled by their craving for art. But to me it's a sign of the desire in Jovials that fuels not only their art but their lives; the desire to bring everyone they love and everything they know to sound one all-inclusive chord. When for a moment they realize this aim they sweep us all along with them and give us a glimpse of some high and illuminating harmony that lies behind our entire world.

The Jovial Type

General Orientation:
Passive-Feminine / Positive

Psychological Overview:
Chief features of vanity, arrogance, control
Maximum attraction of Mercury
Maximum repulsion of Saturn, with whom it competes for
'parental' space; anyone who dares to disagree.

Key Words:
Creative, vain, verbose, grandiose, manipulative,
center-of-attention, kindly, generous, deceitful

Examples:

Walt Whitman	Santa Claus
Burl Ives	Orson Welles
Beverly Sills	Pablo Casals
H. Norman Schwarzkopf	Falstaff

William Benham's Physical Description:
The pure Jovial is of medium height. He is not the tallest of the seven types; that distinction belongs to the Saturn; neither is he the shortest, for this honor belongs to the Mercury. He is, however, a large man, very strongly built and inclined to be fleshy. His flesh is solid and not mere fat, nor does it partake of the spongy softness of the Lunar type. His bones are large, strong, and well able to support his weight. He has a smooth, clear skin, which inclines to be fine in texture, pink in color, and healthy looking. His eyes are large and expressive, pupils are clear and dilate under the play of the emotions. There is no fierce look in his eyes—the expression is mild and almost melting, bespeaking honesty and a kindly spirit. The upper lids of the eyes are thick, looking as if somewhat swollen, and the lashes are long and curl up grace-fully at the ends. The eyebrows are arched and the hairs grow

evenly, giving the brows a clearly defined outline. The nose is straight and well formed, tending to be large in size, and often Roman in shape. The mouth is large, the lips full and red, and owing to the position of the teeth the upper lip is slightly prominent. The teeth are strong and white, but grow long and narrow, the two front teeth being longer than is usual. The cheeks are well rounded, so the cheek bones are not to be seen. The ears are well formed, regular, and set close to the head, which rests on a well-shaped, thick neck of medium length and strong looking. The back and shoulders are fleshy and squarely set. The legs and feet are shapely and of medium size, but strong and firm. The walk is stately and dignified. The hair is brown or running into chestnut; in women of the type, grows long, is abundant and fine in quality, inclining to be curly. The Jovial perspires freely, especially on top of the head, from ordinary exertion. This often leads to baldness early in life.

As he is of a vigorous constitution he has considerable hair on his body, which is a sign of strength. The chest of the Jovial is well developed, and his large lungs are bellows from which is forced a rich, musical voice, which is just the voice to give words of command, or speak to and influence a multitude; helping to make a Jovial the natural leader that he is.

It is not hard to see why such a personality as the Jovial should command followers, for his strong and robust manhood proves attractive, and confidence in his strength at once moves men to desire an alliance with him. He is designed to command; nature has given him the strength and attractiveness that will enable him to secure and to lead followers.

Jovial Circulation

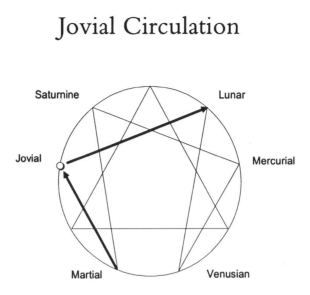

From Conviviality to Coolness

Martial energy lends energy and activity to Jovial as it flows to this point on the enneagram. This activity and masculine energy circulates within the type as it peaks in Jovial, but soon fades away in the move towards Lunar passivity.

Jovial can correct its on-again, off-again interests by acquiring the persistence inherent in Lunar. Its sometimes overflowing feelings—and slavery to those feelings—may be reined in by the discipline and self-abnegation of the Lunar type. When Jovial, overflowing with emotion and likely to soar into abstract realms, needs to come down to earth, they can look toward the pragmatism and practicality of the earth-bound Lunar for assistance.

The danger here is that the Jovial may simply grow cool and distant and, rather than focusing its self-image, grow aloof and isolated. This development ought to be avoided. It can only produce a negative result, and the idea of this progression is to temper the Jovial spirit and make it realistic, not to create a deeply-felt detachment.

Jovial-Lunar

The Jovial-Lunar suggests depth and timidity, vanity with dark humor, a 'soft' or 'airy' type.

Jovial-Lunars will maintain some of the roundness of Jovial amid the thin, watery elements of Lunar. Baldness is likely in men, and the type is not known for its physical vitality. Without the ruddy or vital quality of the more active types, Jovial-Lunars will usually be pale, with a weak chin and perhaps a Jovial paunch.

The combination of feeling with control is ideal for a life in the world of music, art, or literature, and we find many examples of the type in these pursuits. The Jovial capability in the world can also combine with the Lunar genius at secretiveness, and it is not uncommon for Jovial-Lunars to rise in the world of business, but as the proportion of Lunar increases, this direction becomes less and less likely.

Jovial-Lunars frequently confuse us as their personality slips back and forth between seeing society and demanding solitude. They seem a bit schizophrenic, at one moment gushing with enthusiasm and interest about our projects, and the next day barely answering questions. As with every transitional type, it is the inner contradictions that frequently provide the fuel for coming to terms with our various tendencies, and which will also provide the food for our inner growth.

Jovial-Lunars will need to come to terms with both sides of their contradictory character in order to create a positive self-image for themselves.

Examples:

Queen Victoria	Alfred Hitchcock
Wallace Shawn	Diane Ladd
Mikhail Gorbachev	Maurice Nicoll
Bernie Siegal	Joanne Woodward

The Solar Type

Solars fascinate me, as indeed they fascinate everyone who isn't Solar. They are as close as a human can come to passing from material flesh to pure energy. They are to the rest of us what a hummingbird is to other birds; the speed limit of the species. Solars, dashing and dancing about, can make you think their nerves are going to fray from overuse, or that their bones are about to fly apart.

Burning bright and intense, Solars are in constant motion. They dance when they walk and mime while they talk. Their eyes gleam with intensity when you're talking to them. Energy animates their bodies and radiates into the atmosphere around them.

Doesn't Fit Neatly

There's something strange about the Solar type, something not quite right. It doesn't slip comfortably into the scheme of types; you've got to shoe-horn it in. It's a type that lacks the tensions of attraction and repulsion that inflame the other types. Their metabolism must be very different as well, to process fuel the way they do. Their differences are reflected in the enneagram we've used for plotting the course of the other types, but on which Solar doesn't seem to occupy a distinct spot.

In some ways, Solar doesn't look like a distinct type at all, but more like a supercharger that can be fitted onto any of the other types. When you think you've seen a Solar, you've invariably seen other types in the person as well. Separating the Solar from what it's combined with can be difficult, and the effort often proves inconclusive. But the first signs of Solar—no matter where we find them—are excitement, excitation, energy, electricity, vibration and just plain speed.

Lunar-Solars, Saturn-Solars, Venusian-Mercury-Solars, all the Solars are Solar-something, hyphenated types, people with built-in combinations tugging at their varied, and sometimes incompatible, motives. And although we are all divided, unlike the impossibly pure types described in this book, we can usually identify distinct strains of the basic types in ourselves. We can see each type's function, and try to organize these functions into a more complete picture of how we are made.

Solar Affects Each Type

In the study of Solar this process works differently. By being mated to other types Solar yields, for instance, a Jovial, but a revved up one. He's still Jovial, but he's been over-refined, drawn tight. Straight lines and sharp corners have replaced curves and bulges. This Jovial-Solar hybrid smarts easily because his vanity has been raised to a new level of excitation. He's become over-sensitive to criticism, and can't stop entertaining. He's more captivating than an ordinary Jovial, but he's also more distant.

We need to know the traits of Solar to observe the type. But if we want to ferret Solar out, we also need to remember that these traits always combine with the traits of other types.

When you look for Solars, look for them pure and undiluted; but look as well for the color they add to the types with which they combine.

In part because it's so difficult to keep your observation on two different types at once, people have odd ideas about Solar.

Some people will tell you that Solar appears in everybody's body type, no matter how small the dose. These observers measure Solar in parts-per-hundred with an apparently perfect gauge they've got in their minds. Other people claim to see nothing but a distinct type in Solar, one that doesn't mix. They treat Solars like unearthly children, in whose refinement lie the traces of a higher world. These people are awed by Solars, and aren't put off even when their favorites grow demanding.

Prudent Observation is Called For

It's better to be prudent, to go slowly. Get to know the six other types well, and keep Solar in the back of your mind, on call. It will explain many things you will see that you can't otherwise account for; it won't explain everything. If you're interested in learning types, then learn to wait for the recognition that snaps your head back, the shock you get when you really see a type.

The study of types demands that we keep our minds both open and cautious, and this is true nowhere more than in the study of Solar. Solars will enchant and beguile you, they will madden and may enrage you, but they will never bore you.

Solars Energize Us

Solars energize us, even daze us. They make us come alive, and fill us with a nervous excitement. Solars don't seem to represent a particular function of ours, but rather heighten and extend our sensitivity to include a whole new range of impressions; we're quicker when we're around them. This energy accounts for most of the characteristics of Solar, and for the effects they have on everyone else.

Physical Description

Fair-skinned, with wide-set, entrancing eyes, Solars vibrate more quickly than we do. They can charge the atmosphere around them with electricity and anticipation. Brilliant entertainers, their act sails on a wave of intensity, and their energy alone may carry us along for awhile. Solars have that quality of attraction, that personal magnetism some call *charisma*. We are drawn to them, but may not stay long; it's much too difficult to keep up with the rate at which they're burning, and with the flutter of their thoughts.

When they're active Solars are like children whose motives and morals have been transferred to the higher functions of an adult. They're restless, easily captivated and changeable. They always seem to be either on the verge of laughter, or about to swell into tears.

Can Be Similar to Children

Solars yield to the same extreme emotions that children yield to, but with more force. Their tantrums are as teary as a child's, but more elegant. They want a toy to make them feel better just as desperately, but the toy has become a mink coat.

Solars forget themselves the way children do; you have to remind them that it's cold outside, or they simply won't notice they were about to take a walk in a snowstorm without a coat. They skip meals without a thought, and when they become weak, attribute it to the exciting time they've been having. They are delicately made, susceptible to illnesses and ailments of many kinds. They seem as unprotected and unfinished as some of the other kids we know.

In a Fantasy World

Like children, Solars delight in fantasy. But as adults, they can remain unaware of the brutality of life. They inhabit a black-and-white, good-or-evil world built like the world of fairy tales. Theirs is a romantic existence, sketched in dramatic tones. It's a world in which they know that awful dragons lurk in the dark woods, but never doubt that a young prince will reach his breathless, swooning princess just in time to save her.

Dreams maintain this romantic world. Disturbed by the random injustice and gratuitous violence of our world, Solars calm themselves with the dreams of their fantasies. They invest the world they've imagined with purity and goodness and, uplifted, seem to overlook the harsh, the demeaning and the bloody.

A Creative Type

Solars create more than fantasies. Their creativity also emerges in plays and in acting. It combines with their charisma to fashion them into singers and entertainers; you'll find them in all the worlds of make-believe. They are poets of sensitivity and artists with a delicate, rarefied vision.

Their active imagination dresses Solars in costumes designed to produce an effect, or to show which part they're playing today. They make a bright and bold impression in a group, their vibrant energy intensified by their habit of wearing vibrant colors. They prefer an airy, ethereal look, or else a shocking one, and when they aren't looking frilly and feminine they're likely to turn up in conspicuous combinations of red and black.

They Stand Out in a Crowd

You can't help noticing Solars. The delicacy of their looks makes them stand out, and they take it naturally when they are cared for and admired. They're hothouse flowers that wilt without the heat of your attention, and think something must be wrong if you leave them even for a moment. They have no use for your criticism, constructive or otherwise; what they yearn for is your adoration.

Solars puzzle those of us who wonder why, since we're so easily captivated by them, they continue to seek out the crutch of our reassurance to prop themselves up. They glow with beauty and grace: Don't they know they're the objects of our envy? Or that we see in them the ideal prince or princess we dreamed of as children? But they crave approval with a hunger that can't be sated; they'll never cultivate what they need—self-assurance—from the junk food of our flattery.

You might say that Solars are too easily satisfied, that it's not a deep or penetrating understanding they're after, but a simplified one, a version they can repeat to themselves with conviction and assurance. The cut and color of a new dress is enough to inflame what seem their deepest feelings. It's in impressions, in the form and finish of a thing, that they get their thrills. If you become too serious, they sag. They'll wonder why you don't cheer up and may not wait long for you to come around. Their lives are more fun with someone to play with.

Solar Men and Women

You can see Solar women in clusters sometimes, twittering and feinting like high school ballerinas, all gawky limbs and hot-eyed looks. They're talking about shopping or, in certain circles, reciting fairy tales to each other in quivering tones, or telling the stories of their favorite operas.

Solar men are spare and wan, with high thrust foreheads and bright, feverish spots on their opal cheeks. They're romantic poets, or dancers who jolt their audiences with electric leaps and searing glances. Matinee idols and cabaret singers, they throw magnificent rages, stamping their feet in bouts of pique.

No one else would trust some of the people that Solars attract. They put up no resistance to those who crowd around them, and don't discriminate between the good advice they're given and the bad. As a result they're often victimized by seductive business managers, sleazy agents and crooked lawyers.

Greed in Solars

An adolescent greed keeps pace with the rest of their personality and makes Solars sly and guarded. They get tense worrying about whether they'll get a fair share. This is a tension that can make them intrusive, or rude. They think you should make exceptions for them, take their *differentness* into account. Don't you know they need special treatment, and that others are vying to take care of them?

Solars expect to ascend the social ladder, and don't mind the grasping involved to reach its successive rungs. At meals, even Solars who are quiet and tentative may attack their dinner mercilessly, dispatching great heaps of food to fuel their throbbing factory.

Solars practice a naïve control, trying to trick or charm you into helping them. Their attempts at persuasion, however, are often so obvious that you're as likely to be amused by them as irritated. We don't resent Solars for their intrigue or their success, and in spite of their impractical schemes they hold onto their many friends. Solars champion causes that go along with their rosy view of justice, and may select the victims they'll care for by picking the ones they think are the cutest.

Solars live an odd and fretful life, restless and frail, swept by the winds of their passions and the demands of their admirers. They rush hot and fragile through their days, and are liable to exhaust themselves early in life. They don't seem designed to last for a lifetime of toil, or built as if they were meant to attain any great age.

Solars in Art

The highly colored, vibrant personalities of art and opera are frequently Solars. There's the brilliant Renaissance painter and colorist Raphael Sanzio, whose canvases combine the perfection of form with an ethereal air, both elements that we associate with this type. The extreme sensitivity and romanticism in the poetry of John Keats and Percy Shelley, their tragic lives and early deaths, all speak of Solar.

Then there's Giuseppe Verdi's tempestuous Violetta Valery of the opera *La Traviata.* As a character she exhibits all the traits of Solar. Violetta owns mesmerizing beauty and social wit. She has brilliant friends, engages in stormy affairs and lives an opulent life given over entirely to play. The tragical action of the story hinges on her romantic abandon to a world of fantasy that eventually collides, as it must, with the requirements of an unjust and political world. At the end of the opera, it's her fragile constitution that sends her to an early, dramatic and romantic end.

Solar Attractions

A Solar is a positive type, which he demonstrates by his idealism and his optimism. He's active, which we can observe from his abundant energy. But unlike the other types, these characteristics don't limit the people he attracts, or the people to whom he's attracted. He works his magic on all the types, and appeals to us equally. Where we have been identifying active types with masculine energy and passive types with feminine, and finding in these relationships some clue to people's drives, in Solar we can't make the same connection.

This type doesn't seem to take a firm step in either a masculine or feminine direction. Instead, it adds to whatever type it's found with, but with unpredictable results. The Solar influence can make a woman vastly more airy, or shoot her through with ambition; is it masculine or feminine?

Solar rarely primes a man's virility. More often it induces a tremble, or vibrato into his chemistry that's unmistakably feminine. These men become poetic and may lack the vigor it takes to engage in the manly arts of war or conquest. They don't belong in the arena, and their fragile health can undermine their drive for fame.

Solar inflames the metabolism of the people in whom it is found, and produces a surplus of energy. But we can't take this energy and the activity it causes in Solars as masculine. A Solar's drive for sex can be intense, matching the intensity he produces in all his functions. He may find in sex an outlet for the excess energy his body produces, but at times he can also appear to be sexually neutral. Perhaps his attractions have more to do with excitability and a need for company than with the hungers of a Solar's body.

Appearances are Important

Solars spend a lot of time on their costumes, endlessly primping and preening. They log hundreds of hours in front of mirrors, and like to stop for a consultation with the reflections in a store window while walking. They look at themselves so often, and so intensely, that they're usually well-turned out.

They know how to maximize their natural beauty and grace, even if it's at the expense of their humility. Solars have so much concern for their own appearance, and for the look of things in general, that as a type they may come to rely on appearances to an unfortunate degree.

A Solar wants to latch onto simple solutions, even for those problems where the simple won't suffice. If he's presented with a belief spelled out in a few syllables, he's tempted to catch hold of it and never think that he's missed something hidden, or worry about its implications. Complicated arguments are confusing and cloud his mood, and he doesn't care for the shadow they throw over him. He'll bunch his brows if you present him with a knotty problem, and work himself into a gloomy lassitude.

Luckily this mood won't hold him long. You may see a Solar deep in a funk, but he's easily revived, and his sense of play can break through almost any dark moment. Then he rises, ready for an escapade, and once again his eyes sparkle and his cheeks are flushed. Cares are forgotten with the promise of adventure and clouds are swept away by another feverish round of activity. Soon he's spinning through the room from friend to friend, showering everyone with his radiance and for a few moments he dazzles our more ordinary eyes with his unearthly and beautiful light, and then he's gone.

The Solar Type

General Orientation:
Active-Androgynous / Positive

Psychological Overview:
Chief features of vanity, manipulation, naïveté
No particular *Maximum attraction*
No particular *Maximum repulsion*

Key Words:
Light, airy, energetic, electric, fine, doomed, vibrating,
androgynous, manipulative, childish, naïve, self-destructive

Examples:

Judy Garland	Liza Minelli
Prince	Michael Jackson
Madonna	Iman
Rudolph Nureyev	

William Benham's Physical Description:
The Solar is a handsome and a manly type. He is of medium height, between the Jovial and Saturn, is not fleshy like the Jovial nor lean and lanky like the Saturn, but is shapely, muscular, and athletic. The lines of the body run in graceful curves, and he is light and supple. His complexion is clear, his skin white, fine and firm in texture, and cheeks rosy. This pinkness of color gives the clue to a healthy condition and consequent attractiveness. The hair is thick, wavy, and black or auburn in color, fine and silky in quality, and when he has a beard it partakes of the same fineness and abundance, growing over the chin, lip, and high on the cheeks. His forehead is broad and full, but not high, the eyes are large, almond-shaped, brown or blue in a frank, honest expression, which changes to sweetness and sympathy when the emotions are in play, and they sparkle with the brilliancy and life of the brain behind them. His cheeks are firm and rounded, showing

no hollows. The nose is straight and finely shaped, the nostrils beautifully proportioned, and dilating sensitively under the play of emotions; as is the case with all highly strung organizations. The mouth is graceful in outline, the lips curved and set evenly, neither thin nor large and thick. The teeth are finely shaped, strong, even, and white, firmly set in healthy red gums. The chin is shapely and rounded, neither retreating nor protruding, showing evenly balanced firmness. The ears are of medium size, well formed, and pink, setting close to the head. The neck is long, muscular, and well shaped, but showing neither cord-like muscles, nor a prominent 'Adam's apple.' This shapely neck connects the well shaped head with strong shoulders, which are muscular and graceful. The chest is full and capacious, expands well under the inspiration, which fact undoubtedly contributes much to purifying the blood, pink color with healthy conditions following. The voice is musical, but not full or resonant. The lower limbs are graceful, muscular, finely proportioned, and are never fat. The feet are of medium size, the insteps arching and high, which gives spring and elasticity to the walk. This is a particularly distinguishing feature of the Solar. In this type is a picture of healthy conditions, beautiful proportions, grace and symmetry of body, and to these must be linked a mind full of similar charms and attributes. From every point of view the Solar is brilliant, full of the love of beauty, art, color, and form.

Solar Circulation

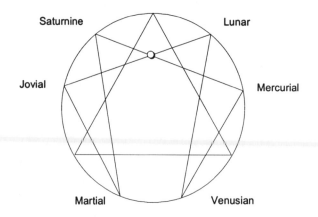

Solar is a type that combines with every other type on the enneagram. In each case, it adds something of its own, to a greater or lesser degree, and changes the type accordingly. For example, the Saturn-Solar may be even further elongated, more attenuated than the Saturn usually is. At the same time, this type will find its breadth of view invested with fantasy and naïveté, rather than pragmatic planning, as a 'pure' Saturn might. As another example, a Solar-Mars is a kind of hyped-up version of Mars, electric with energy and vibrating at an incredible speed. In each case the basic attributes of the type are supercharged, rather than superseded, by the addition of the Solar element, whatever it is.

There is no known circulation for Solar. However, since Solar almost always appears in combination with the other types, one can rely on the ordinary circulation on the enneagram for guidance in progressive evolution.

The most pressing need of Solar, however, from the point of view of this continued development, is to acquire a realistic idea of themselves first of all. By eliminating the elements of fantasy that work their way into a Solar's idea of themselves, they can begin to use their abundant energy for constructive ends.

PART III

Additional Information

Gods and Planets

Although we cannot say when the planets were named for the chief gods of the most ancient religions, their names have been linked since the dawn of civilization. However, we do know that while the primitive study of astronomy was gradually becoming more specialized, it was at the same time growing closer and closer to religion.

These early religions gave birth, in turn, to various mythologies that fueled our ancestors' efforts in literature, science, philosophy, art and education. The gods and goddesses, whose actions had long been called on to explain an enigmatic world, were eventually joined to the planets, and planet and god became one.

Three Independent Systems

Body types connects these gods and their planets with human types and with the glands of the endocrine system. By doing so it gives us a new angle on some very old knowledge. The merging of mythological gods and medieval alchemy with modern astronomy and endocrinology provides us with the possibility of an entirely new way to understand man as an orderly part of an entire system.

In the study of body types this scrutiny progresses in two fields from two points of view. We see each endocrine gland as the ruler of a particular group of biological functions, and also as an integral part of a complete system of functions. We study the gods and goddesses in the same way, trying to extract from our observations an idea of the unique function each personifies in the whole scheme of human activity, while also trying to determine the position each god and goddess occupies in the pantheon of the gods. These parallels continue in the study of the solar system, where individual planets vary to a great degree, yet form a cohesive whole, complete and harmonious.

From the picture we build up by these observations we plot the coordinates that connect not just the glands, gods and planets, but those that indicate the shape of men as well. The pattern in which these studies are combined is reminiscent of the fabric of human society. Although we can look for correspondences among these very different worlds, we can't expect a simple and symmetrical picture to come from glands, gods or planets any more than we can expect it from our uncles, friends or peers.

The Universe

The planets we relate to body types are the sun, moon, Mercury, Venus, Mars, Jupiter and Saturn. These are the objects that have always been visible in our skies. They dominate our myths and have given their names to the human types. They themselves exist within the whirling phenomena of the astronomical universe.

When we try to describe the universe we run into a peculiar problem: we're unable to comprehend the numbers used to describe it. For instance, the universe is supposed to be about 13 billion (13,000,000,000) years old. Now try to imagine the age it may eventually attain. Stretches that are measured in billions of years don't describe to me a length of time; they tell me about our inability to comprehend them. Their immensity removes them from the scope of our understanding.

As the universe expands—which it seems to be doing—perhaps every piece of 'space' and every location in 'time' stretches as well, changing imperceptibly the very weave of 'reality.' Even when we attempt to study the objects that populate the universe—the largest of which are galaxies—we're left just as puzzled by our knowledge.

Galaxies are the citizens of the visible and energetic universe. Astronomers have estimated that there are 100 billion individual galaxies, each containing billions of stars. These amalgams of dust, gas and stars are held together by their own gravitational force, and are simultaneously being pulled apart by the force of their spin as they rotate through space.

We don't know how galaxies relate to the universe as a whole, or whether they all revolve around the same center. We see them gathered into clusters in which individual galaxies are still distinct. A 'typical' galaxy is a disc about 100,000 light years in diameter. This means that the flash of a star at one end of the disc, travelling at the speed of light, would take a thousand centuries to reach the other side of its own galaxy.

Our Sun

Within the 100 billion stars that constitute the Milky Way—our galaxy—our sun lies some 30,000 light years from the galaxy's center; it takes 200 million years to complete one orbit around the galactic core.

The star that animates our family of planets may be 4,560 million years old. During that time the sun somehow created or captured the planets that have evolved into a coherent system of satellites, and which still circle it. While astronomers and physicists have learned a great deal about the evolution of stars, the forces responsible for this evolution remain obscure. We can't see far enough or well enough to study the laws and principles involved in this process—they're simply beyond our reach.

Our sun, like all stars, generates energy and power at tremendous heat and crushing pressures, conditions that lie well beyond our imagination. Nevertheless, men have connected the light and heat generated by our star with its evolution, and perhaps for that reason have seen in the sun the embodiment of our own highest functions: thought, awareness and love.

The sun is an astounding creation. It's a huge gaseous globe more than 100 times the size of the Earth. It has more than a million times the volume of the Earth and more than 330,000 times the mass, but it's only one-quarter as dense. The sun's fiery core reaches temperatures of up to 20 million degrees centigrade. It also contains every element found on Earth. Virtually all of the mass of its entire system of planets, asteroids, satellites, comets, dust clouds and random debris, in fact, is contained within the brilliant ball of the sun.

The sun has usually been called Sol, and may have been known at an earlier time as Uranus. Occasionally the Greeks called it Hyperion, but to them it was most of all Apollo, the sun-god.

Like many of the other Greek gods and their Roman descendants, Apollo doesn't seem to play a role in the scheme of types. But the cultural and religious qualities of other ancient gods parallel the qualities of the planets that bear their names. And the gods and planets taken together possess uncanny similarities to their namesakes among the planetary types.

The Moon

Selene drove the chariot that carried the moon across the sky and she was goddess of the moon for the ancient Greeks. The Romans called her Luna. She is often mentioned along with Artemis, a primitive goddess who protected women, brought fertility to the farms of the people and ruled uncultivated land and forests.

Artemis was known as a 'lion unto women.' She was a virgin, the goddess of birth and she slew the hunter Orion. She was the daughter of Zeus and Apollo's sister. Artemis was also a huntress—she's often shown in sculptures and paintings draped with the skins of her prey.

In a later age we find the attributes of Artemis being appropriated by Diana, an ancient Italian deity of the woods, of women and of fertility. Diana originally lacked a clear connection to the moon but the passage of time blended Selene, Luna, Artemis and Diana into one image. Today it's Diana that comes to mind when we think of the huntress who is goddess of the silvery orb of the moon. Diana was both moody and persistent. In these two traits she resembles the Earth's satellite, which passes through moody phases, but which also accompanies us as our regular and constant companion.

The Earth and Moon have sometimes been called a 'double planet.' Compared to the other moons in our solar system, ours is certainly closer and more nearly equal in size to the Earth than any of the other moons are to the planets that they circle.

The moon's size and distance are such that a precise, mathematical coincidence of the strangest variety takes place each time it moves into alignment between the Earth and the sun. To observers on Earth during these alignments—called solar eclipses—the disc of the moon appears to be exactly the size of the disc of the sun. Consequently, as the moon swings in front of the sun, it blocks it out completely.

While even the largest satellites of Jupiter and Saturn are nowhere near as large as their hosts, our moon is much closer to the size, density and volume of the Earth. For instance, the moon is about one-quarter the size of the Earth. Jupiter's Ganymede, one of the largest moons in the solar system, is barely a thirtieth the size of its host.

Our moon travels through an elliptical orbit 240,000 miles away from us. It has become so dependent on the Earth that its revolution has come to equal its own rotation. Because of these identical movements, as the moon wheels and spins through our skies, it shows only one side of itself to us on the Earth.

Although the moon retains its aura of mystery by remaining eternally half-hidden, it influences us throughout its phases. Its gravity pulls and releases us as it waxes and wanes, just as it pulls and releases the oceans, creating spring and neap tides each month. The moon seems to act on the human body, which is almost as watery as the oceans. It echoes women's menstrual cycles, and each month it reputedly drives many people to lunatic or violent actions.

The moon may have an iron core but it has a weak magnetic field, no atmosphere and no weather. Because it lacks the protection of a gaseous atmosphere it offers no resistance to the dust, debris and passing protons and electrons of the solar winds that bombard it. No water flows on the moon, and no forms of life grow there.

Some see in the moon a child of Earth; some, Earth's captive. But it's our steadfast attendant and, in many of its movements, predictable. Because it reflects so much of the sun's light the Romans associated it with Jupiter, their early sky-god, whom they worshipped during the full moon. The brightness of the full moon added to that of the sun, created a time in each month when there was the most light emanating from the sky.

The moon's unearthly chill has always implied to men the secret whispers of our own dark thoughts. It seems to advocate hidden schemes, to promote madness and to champion shadowy sleep like that of Endymion, Selene's lover. The moon's intimate relationship to the Earth's magnetic and gravitational fields makes it our partner. Perhaps it collects the energy the Earth scatters into space; perhaps it passes its own influence back to us by a method we haven't yet observed. But the Earth and the moon are definitely bound in some special, unique relation.

Venus

As he had with Artemis, Zeus makes another contribution to the pantheon of gods with Aphrodite, his daughter. She was honored for hundreds of years as the goddess of beauty, fertility and love. She was raised from the sea, loved the warrior Ares and bore Aeneas after copulating with the mortal Anchises. She championed Anchises' tribe—the

Trojans—and took their side in an epic war with the Athenians, as recounted by Homer.

Aphrodite was sexuality, and she was love. On occasion prostitutes could be hired in her temples—perhaps due to an overly literal translation of her role in the arts of love. The myrtle was sacred to Aphrodite, as was the dove. She was the goddess of the sea, which had borne her and, by extension, the goddess of sailors. Aphrodite's honors were absorbed by Venus who had been, until that time, an obscure Italian goddess of vegetable nature and fertility.

Artists throughout history have found some of their favorite subjects in Venus' often blatant sexuality, and in the wars of love she waged with Mars. Poets have seen her sexuality as a sign of creative and procreative powers, likening it to a cosmic force that pervades nature. She is represented by the planet that is nearer to us than any other, the brightest planet in our sky and the planet that is the most similar to the Earth.

Venus, perfectly round and white, is closer to the sun than any planet except Mercury and has the most circular orbit of all the planets. The Chinese called it *Tai-pe,* 'beautiful white one.' To the Babylonians it was *Ishtar,* 'bright torch of heaven.' Venus' soft, pearly appearance is produced by the sunlight that reflects off its dense layers of cloud, and which veil it from the Earth.

At one time Venus may have had oceans. If it did, they were boiled off as the sun gradually grew hotter, steaming the planet and creating what is now a kind of super greenhouse. The atmosphere, over 50 miles of haze on top of clouds on top of haze, covers a planet where the 'air' exerts ninety times the pressure as on Earth. Its surface is strewn with rocks, boulders and shale-like stones. Although Venus' density is almost identical to the Earth's, its magnetic field, which is like the electromagnetic signature of a planet, is very weak.

Time on Venus is peculiar, but not because of its year; it takes about 225 of our days for Venus to circle the sun, while it takes the Earth 365 days. But its rotation, which accounts for day and night on the surface of the planet, is very slow.

Drifting along, actually rotating in the opposite direction to the other planets, Venus takes over 20 of our days to make it through one complete spin.

Venus is very slow and very hot, and is bathed in a great deal more of the sun's radiation than we are. Beautiful and serene, it hides its late hour pursuits. Venus is never observable the whole night, losing itself in the angles of our respective orbits. In many ways it remains a languorous, lovely and indistinct mystery.

Mercury

The phallus was the characteristic emblem of Hermes, one of the youngest of the Olympians. While his primitive origins are demonstrated by this emblem of fertility, his cunning is evident everywhere. On the first day of his life Hermes invented the lyre, robbed his brother Apollo and then was reconciled with him—a quick study. He was the messenger for the gods and especially for Zeus, his father, and he carried their symbol on his errands, the caduceus of bound rods.

Hermes was widely known in the ancient world by primitive stone columns, called herms, which featured a young man's curly-haired head carved at the top, sometimes with a winged hat set on his head, and sometimes, sticking out half-way down the column, an enormous, erect penis.

Mercurius, the Roman god of traders and those who travelled the roads, became associated with Hermes the messenger and gathered his traits as well. He became the god of thieves, the god of the oratorical arts and the god of athletic young men. He was also the patron of literature. We see Hermes' most mysterious role when he serves as attendant and guide to the souls he accompanies on their journey after death. In this capacity he carries the magic wand of the necromancer.

Mercury had little interest in morals or philosophy and almost none in civic responsibility. His concerns revolved around himself. He had the same amoral isolation as a child enclosed within his own world. Perhaps it was the elusive quickness of the messenger, the same quickness that flashes through the Mercurial type, that allied him to the swiftest planet.

Mercury's closeness to the sun makes it seem like a child tagging behind its parent in the sky, and also makes it a planet that is difficult to observe because we're usually looking at it against the backdrop of the sun's glare. It moves across the ball of the sun only in its crescent phase, when it's no more than a sliver. It passes behind the sun when it's full, and very close to the sun when it's in front and observable. We can't ever see Mercury clearly, against a wholly dark background, and can only observe it in fleeting moments. Even then it's obscured.

The heavily cratered surface of Mercury is constantly bombarded by solar radiation and by the intensity of the solar wind. With no atmosphere its temperatures are extreme, ranging from 90 to 600 degrees Kelvin. Most of Mercury's magnetic field is thought to have been blown away by the intense radiation of the sun. Now it's only about one-hundredth as strong as the magnetic field of the Earth.

A third the size of Earth but with 95% less mass, Mercury revolves around the sun in a year that lasts only 88 earth days. Its orbit is the most eccentric in the solar system except for Pluto. Both the evolution and the inner composition of the planet remain a mystery. Mercury is so difficult to observe that we'll have to wait for further exploration to penetrate the riddles of this hot, erratic and arid planet.

Saturn

One of the most perverse tales in mythology is the history of the world's beginnings and the rise of the gods as it is recounted by the Greeks. In this story Kronos, youngest son of Heaven and Earth and leader of the Titans, his fellow gods, castrates his father on his mother's advice; she wanted to prevent him from producing any more competition.

Kronos marries his sister Rhea and sires what will become the Olympian gods: Hestia; Demeter, the most important figure in the Eleusinian Mysteries; Hera, Olympian queen; Hades, God of the underworld; Poseidon, ocean ruler; and Zeus.

Kronos, still ridding himself of unwanted competition, did nothing to hurt his vicious reputation by eating all these children except Zeus, who was smuggled out of harm's reach by his mother. Rhea then managed to get Kronos to regurgitate her other children who, led by Zeus, went on to conquer their father and preside over both heaven and earth from their home on Mount Olympus.

This story of warring gods and the cosmic events surrounding Kronos melted into the attributes of the Roman

Saturnus, god of harvests, who also had the merriest festival of the year dedicated to him each December.

Saturnus governed seeds and their sowing and, after the fall of the Titans, came down to Italy to teach the natives agriculture and thereby to civilize them. In joining the unpleasant Kronos with their own ancient god Saturnus, the Latin myth makers captured the grandest aspects of both, and it is the grandest planet of our solar system that bears his name.

Saturn, almost ten times as far from the sun as the Earth, is the last of the inner planets and stands on the edge of the immense distances that stretch from the center of the solar system to Uranus, Neptune and Pluto. Second in size only to Jupiter, it passes through, and may be affected by, the long tail of Jupiter's vast magnetic field. Its mass, also second only to Jupiter's, is almost a hundred times the Earth's and is voluminous enough to contain more than seven hundred planets the size of Earth.

A great gaseous giant, Saturn seems to be composed principally of hydrogen and helium, the same that make up Jupiter, but differently mixed. Its atmosphere is topped by a muted haze that covers multi-colored layers of methane, ammonia and sulphur clouds. It spins amazingly fast, and its day only lasts a little over 10 hours. But the grandest aspect of Saturn, its true insignia, is the incredible system of rings of ice and rock that orbits along with the planet and reaches 50,000 miles beyond the cloud tops of Saturn's atmosphere.

The rings of Saturn have taught astronomers a great deal about the planet's satellites. We know of more than 20 satellites circling Saturn, the biggest array supported by any planet. Most of them are nothing more than frozen rocks. Titan, the largest, is the only moon in the solar system with its own atmosphere. From the evidence of the rings and from periodic radio emissions that it produces, astronomers have deduced that some evolutionary process may be occurring on Saturn. These radio emissions take place with an odd, metronomic regularity, a radio-electric pulse once a day, at noon—Saturn time.

Saturn also has a massive magnetic field, 1,000 times larger than Earth's, which may be the offshoot of an unobserved energy cycle. Maybe some of these familiar planets will someday become stars themselves, roaring through the galaxy with their own planetary systems. It's easy to picture the majestic, immense Saturn as one of these nascent suns.

Mars

Yet another branch of the tree of Zeus is Ares, the Greek warrior god. He was an unlovely god who, like Hermes, had no essential moral functions. To the ancients Ares didn't stand simply for war, which they waged to conquer territory or to defend their homes. What they saw in him was everything bloody and brutal that went with war.

It was Ares who instigated vicious acts, who fell into tempestuous loves, who sired ferocious, violent and outrageous sons and who supported foreign foes like the Trojans, or unusually warlike ones like the Amazons. Aphrodite was his common companion and the mother of two of his children. He had no concern for right or wrong on the battlefield and, even to those who worshipped him, he was an unpopular god.

Ferocious in aspect, courageous in action, Ares easily became associated with Mars, one of the oldest Italian gods, whose power was second only to Jupiter's. His primitive nature encompassed the fields of agriculture and the fields of war, and on both of which he strove to protect the native lands.

The wolf—who gave succor to his son Romulus—is sacred to Mars, as is the woodpecker. Many festivals and competitions were held in his honor in Rome, and he also became the god of the state as the empire became more military.

The planet Mars is his worthy namesake. To us Mars is red in the night sky; we call it the *angry* planet. In this angry aspect of Mars, and in his inflamed and florid features, we recognize his planet.

Mars is the first planet beyond the orbit of the Earth and appears brighter than all others except Venus, his consort, who lies between the Earth and the sun. Mars travels an orbit so eccentric and extreme that, during its closest approach to the sun, the heat it receives varies by as much as 40 percent. Its distance from the sun varies as well, getting as much as twenty percent closer or farther away during a year that lasts 20 of our earthly months.

Mars is about one-third the size of the Earth. It is the least dense of the planets and has a weak magnetic field more like our moon's. Its thin atmosphere—dominated by carbon dioxide—stretches over a chaotic terrain of sand dunes and icy rocks, canyons ten times the size of the Grand Canyon and gigantic volcanoes 16 miles tall. Dense clouds whip themselves into cyclones in this hostile environment, volcanoes erupt and landslides thunder through the mountains. Occasionally the most impressive storms in the solar system blow up on Mars, sending furious clouds of dust sweeping over the planet and darkening it for months.

The obvious change of seasons on Mars, the markings that look like channels or canals, and its proximity to the

Earth have regularly excited the minds of observers, but it displays no evidence of life. Its only moons are two odd, misshapen rocks that have no more sign of life on their surface than does Mars. They are named for Phobos and Deimos, who were the war god's children and his charioteers. Fittingly enough, their names mean fear and rout.

Jupiter

In agricultural societies, man's difficulties as well as the bounty of his harvests seemed to him to come through the agency of the sky and its weather. In primitive religions the sky itself is usually reserved as an attribute for the most potent god of the local pantheon. For the Greeks, Zeus combined all their ancient sky-gods with the warrior who had defeated and imprisoned Kronos and the other Titans, bringing to Earth a new reign. Zeus in turn was credited with siring a host of the most important Olympians: Athena, Artemis, Apollo, Ares and Dionysus among them. His loves were many and his incestuous marriage to his sister Hera was sometimes stormy.

After the battle to overthrow the Titans, retold fantastically by Hesiod, the rule of the world was divided in three parts; Zeus' brothers Hades and Poseidon ruled over Hell and the seas, while Zeus himself held sway over heaven and earth. Zeus is an ancient fertility god who copulated with goddesses, nymphs and mortals, spawning characters that criss-cross the convoluted and inbred world of Greek mythology. Zeus guarded the family and was worshipped in connection with almost every side of Greek life.

Zeus ruled by might rather than by righteousness over a squabbling fraternity of gods and goddesses. Even so, he is the protector of the laws and of the king and, despite his harsh character, he also guards political freedom and public morals. Zeus could erupt as Thunderous Zeus when he rewarded the good or punished the evil. The stoic philosophers recognized in Zeus the principle of fiery reason, which they took to be the highest in the universe, and which they thought pervaded and animated all of creation.

When the Greek gods were woven into the Roman pantheon, Zeus was naturally transformed into Jupiter, an old Italian sky god. The Romans worshipped Jupiter at the full moon and made him responsible for weather and thunderstorms. Jupiter presided at the triumphs of generals and protected treaties and oaths. He was the son and conqueror of Saturn, cager of the Titans and sire of the Roman equivalent of Zeus's children. The worship of Jupiter developed into a glittery cult with many festivals and rites. It's fitting that the greatest of gods is symbolized by the fifth planet, the tremendous gaseous giant of Jupiter.

Next to the ringed glory of Saturn, Jupiter is the most visually startling planet. It's a multicolored ball of flowing winds and gas that roil its atmosphere of hydrogen, helium, methane, ammonia gas and ammonia crystals. Unknown forces on Jupiter have created incredible atmospheric effects, among them a bright red oval spot some 30,000 miles long. Composed primarily of liquids, Jupiter spins so fast that its gaseous globe has flattened somewhat at the poles and bulged at the equator. It completes a rotation about once every 10 hours.

The development of Jupiter has somehow made it by far the most massive planet in the Solar System. Two-thirds of all the mass of all the planets, their moons, rings and dust, belongs to Jupiter; it's well over 300 times as massive as the Earth.

Jupiter is surrounded by at least 16 satellites as well as a faint system of rings. One of these satellites—Ganymede—is the solar system's largest moon; it's slightly larger than the planet Mercury. The four largest Jovian moons are so huge that Galileo was able to discover them using only his seventeenth-century instruments. Heavily-cratered Callisto and strangely reflective Europa are also large, but Jupiter has the most interesting relationship with the closest of the four, the enigmatic Io.

Jupiter produces the largest, most powerful magnetic field of all the planets. It manufactures energy in a process that seems to be speeding up as Jupiter becomes less and less dense. It throws off intense, fluctuating radio signals and has created what is in effect an enormous dynamo, with Io as a moving part. Jupiter appears to some astronomers to be connected to Io by a 'tube' of electrical energy that pulses with seventy times the generating capacity of all the powerplants on Earth.

Whether this mechanism controls, escalates or regulates Jupiter's complex magnetic field and huge radiation belts is uncertain, but it may affect the electromagnetic radiation produced by the planet. The radio signals it produces last anywhere from a few minutes to several hours. These signals sometimes indicate that bursts of cosmic rays and trapped particles are being flung from Jupiter's magnetic field so forcefully that they're travelling at close to the speed of light.

The most fascinating coincidence in the analogy between planets and people is connected to these Jovian forces, and to the changes they are working over enormous spans of time. These changes, which seem to reveal Jupiter as a planet that's on its way to becoming a star, are parallel to drastic changes that may occur for men as well.

It's at Jupiter's position on the enneagram that the flow of types, which has been endlessly coursing through their fixed points, can jump to a new level. At this point Jupiter's evolution from planet to star becomes an image representative of human evolution. It's an image that suggests a possibility for man that's as new and as radical as Jupiter's transformation would be; the possibility that a man might become a self-generating, illuminating and energizing individual. That he could become a man who is himself poised, like Jupiter, on the threshold of a transcendental rebirth.

Glands and Behavior

Extending throughout the human body is a network of specialized glands that controls much of our behavior by sending minute amounts of hormones as messengers into our blood. They are called the *endocrine* (ductless) glands, and they regulate many of our basic physiological processes: metabolism, growth, reproduction and the maintenance of the body's internal environment. Our survival, both as individuals and as a species, depends on these glands' proper functioning.

The glands in the endocrine system are the posterior and anterior pituitary, hypothalamus, thyroid, parathyroid, adrenal cortex and adrenal medulla, islands of Langerhans in the pancreas, female ovaries and male testes, the placenta in pregnant women and the pineal body, which is lodged in the brain just behind the hypothalamus. The entire endocrine system is a complex mechanism that relies on the fact that the functioning of its individual glands often contradict each other. This opposition, inherent in their work, enables them to balance many of the body's functions.

The endocrine glands play a special part in the theory of body types, in which some of the correspondences invented by the medieval alchemists have been borrowed, modified and then applied to the endocrine glands. The result is that each of these glands is presumed to be an instrument tuned to the frequency of a corresponding planet, with which it is associated. This particular sensitivity allows each gland to be some kind of ideal 'receptor' for the influences apparently 'broadcast' in some unknown way by the appropriate planet.

Medical science still lacks a complete knowledge of the endocrine glands. Although researchers can observe them more critically, and measure their functions more precisely than ever, these observations and measurements have only succeeded in producing new questions rather than definite answers. Even some functions of the glands remain a mystery.

The endocrine system keeps a constant watch over the levels of different hormones in the blood as they circulate, in turn, through each gland. Each gland is sensitive to particular hormones and, when an imbalance of that hormone occurs, the appropriate gland will sense this, and react.

The action the gland will take is usually to discharge a hormone of its own into the bloodstream. Usually, this hormone calls on the body to produce a substance that will correct the imbalance. Endocrine cells produce hormones that are carried in the blood to target cells. These hormones not only carry the gland's message, they are themselves the message, and they find their targets in an ingenious way.

Like a key cut to fit the path of a lock, each of these cells is designed to 'dock' with a target cell that is constructed to be the exact opposite of the message cell. Through this marvelous bit of chemical engineering the endocrine glands quicken, retard and maintain the enzyme activity in the target cells. It's easy to see why it has been said that all body functions can ultimately be reduced to cellular functions.

Cells

Our bodies contain about 30 trillion cells. To get an idea of the variety of the cells that make up our bodies, look at your arm. Try to imagine a square drawn on your skin, one inch on a side.

If your eyes were acute enough to survey the cells in this plot of familiar real estate, they would see there 500 sweat glands, over 1,000 nerve endings, yards of blood vessels, almost 100 oil glands, 150 sensors to register pressure, heat and cold, and millions of cells. The drop of blood spilled when you cut yourself shaving contains about 5 million red blood cells.

Cells are the smallest individual entities in our body. They are capable of reproducing themselves and, in the process, of passing along the complex codes and ciphers that determine our genetic inheritance. They form the smallest building blocks of the body, massing together into tissues and then taking on the life of the tissues they have become. Cells come in quite an assortment of sizes. The largest is the ovum, or egg, produced by menstruating women, which is one twenty-fifth of an inch. The smallest cells are only one thousandth that size.

How the Glands Work

The endocrine glands constantly measure the ingredients in the blood and of the fluid between the cells in order to carry out their functions. Some regulate the metabolism of food, fuel and the availability of other necessary ingredients. Some determine the body's rate of growth and development. Others determine our sexual rhythms and affect the specialized chemistry and functions of reproduction. Endocrine secretions also control the body's electrical balance, its temperature and the rate at which it burns energy.

The glands somehow manage to execute all these complex responsibilities with great accuracy. They do it amidst changes taking place at every moment as we pass from one state of mind to another, from attentive study to surprise, to chagrin. Because our chemical make-up changes constantly in response to each moment's changing conditions, the hormone levels in our bodies vary continually. At every moment survival depends on the endocrine system making precise readings of stimuli and situations, and making appropriate responses.

How do the glands manage it? They affect every one of the body's systems, each of which can be looked at as a group of related functions. The endocrine system itself influences the skeletal, muscular, circulatory, digestive, respiratory, urinary and reproductive systems. It's controlled, in turn, by the nervous system. In other words, the glands are managed by the brain, and are simply one of the vehicles used by the nervous system to keep us alive.

The Nervous System

Our nervous system decides when we will act and when we will react; it's our ruling faculty. It gives rise to primitive rage and to religious ecstasy. Of its millions of nerve cells—or neurons—one half function as collectors of information from throughout the body. These neurons are concentrated in our sense organs, where they've become specialized, and gather in our spinal cord, along which they relay their information by minute electrical and chemical signals to the other half—the brain.

The language of the nervous system is electro-chemical. Highway signs, today's breakfast and the whispers of love are stimuli that eventually become chemical signals, which are in turn somehow converted into electricity and back into chemical replies. We have no way of explaining the mechanism whereby a neuron produces a minute electrical charge that leaps across space to another, outreaching neuron. Nor can we explain the translation of the physical shunting of chemicals from one place to another into invisible electric charges.

We can, however, trace the effects of this process. We can follow the flow of these chemical signals along the circuitous paths they follow to terminals in muscles and glands. And in so doing, we can watch the formation of a response to the initial stimulus.

These transactions are performed by peripheral nerves. Among these are the autonomic nerves, a subsidiary system that receives and transmits messages regulating the iris, along with the muscles of the heart, lungs, stomach and the glands.

Lying deep in the brain between the midbrain and the cerebrum, and just below the thalamus, is the hypothalamus. It is the hypothalamus—agent for the autonomic nervous system—that relays impulses along the chain of neurons in the spinal cord and moves them to muscles and glands all over the body. Through these impulses it directly or indirectly controls many of our organs, our heartbeat, respiration, the opening and closing of blood vessels and the tightening of the stomach and intestines.

The nerve cells of the hypothalamus also produce hormones which they introduce into the body through the posterior part of the pituitary gland. This little-known gland has no actual secretions of its own, yet seems to play a unique role in the endocrine cycle.

Usually each of the endocrine glands secretes hormones which it produces. But the posterior pituitary—which releases the hormones that are created in the hypothalamus—doesn't appear to create any hormones of its own. But because it is connected to the hypothalamus by its stem, the posterior pituitary seems to form a bridge between the world of the glands and the more rarefied world of the brain.

The hypothalamus also sends hormones directly into the blood through the network of nerves that links the brain with the spinal cord. Via this roundabout route it controls the anterior pituitary, which in turn affects many of the other endocrine glands, and effectively rules the internal balance of the human body.

The Pancreas and the Lunar Body Type

We begin our tour of the endocrine glands in the pancreas, the gland associated with the Lunar body type. The pancreas is important to the process of digestion and has some connection to the lymphatic system. It is considered an endocrine gland because of its clumps of hormone-producing cells, known as the islands of Langerhans. Although bits of cellular activity account for only a small percentage of the cells in the pancreas, they do produce several important hormones.

Insulin, one of the hormones produced by the islands of Langerhans, lowers the level of sugar in the blood. Glucagon, another, raises it. These opposite effects are produced, in the first instance, by stimulating the liver to produce more glucose. In the second, they're produced by increasing the rate at which energy is burned in the cells, effectively reducing the overall glucose level.

The islands of Langerhans also manufacture somatostatin, which is found in many other areas of the body as well. This hormone affects the movement of nutrients from the digestive system into the blood and may slow the body's absorption of those nutrients.

These associations of the Lunar type with the maintenance of burnable fuel in the carbohydrate chain aren't mentioned in the theory of body types. Instead, Lunar is seen as a 'watery' type because of the pancreas' connection to the lymphatic system. This system carries essential nutrients acquired from the digestion of food to the blood in our veins. The blood then carries these nutrients to cells throughout the body.

An abundance of lymph is said to be responsible for the Lunar's round and limpid appearance. However, if there is a connection between the pancreas and the lymphatic system, it remains largely unknown to contemporary endocrinology. An explanation has not yet been found for this apparent contradiction, in which the pancreas—and by extension the passive, inert Lunar type—is firmly connected to the cycle of energy production.

The Parathyroid and the Venusian Body Type

Venus is associated with the parathyroids. Actually four small glands that weigh about an ounce each, they sit on the corners of the thyroid gland. The parathyroids produce parathormone (PTH), which opposes and balances calcitonin, a hormone produced by the thyroid. PTH increases the rate at which calcium and phosphorus move from the bones into the bloodstream. It also acts to retain more calcium in the kidneys and digestive system as a whole, which is then passed into the bloodstream.

This balance of calcium is critical to us; it allows the impulses coming from our nerves to move our muscles. The secretion of PTH is controlled by the parathyroids, which monitor the blood and constantly measure its level of calcium. A lack of calcium produces dire symptoms that are the opposite of the lethargic Venusian body type's habits; muscle spasms, over-excitability and nervousness that can bring a person close to death.

Over-activity of the parathyroids produces too much calcium and may eventually soften and deform the bones; it also causes calcium and water to be lost in our urine. These actions of the parathyroids on calcium levels in the blood don't necessarily reinforce the picture we have of the earthy, sluggish Venusian type. Perhaps more knowledge is yet to be uncovered about this gland and its essential work.

The Thyroid and the Mercurial Type

The thyroid, about an ounce of tissue in two lobes joined by an isthmus, straddles the windpipe; it is the gland of Mercury. It is roused to activity by the hypothalamus and the anterior pituitary. One of its hormones—calcitonin— lowers the calcium level of the blood and works in opposition to the parathyroids. But another of its secretions, called the thyroid hormone, affects us in more wide-ranging and more dramatic ways.

The thyroid hormone controls the activity of enzymes which in turn control the speed at which energy is consumed in the body's cells. Through this control it affects all processes that require the combustion of energy, including growth. Its effects are monitored in the bloodstream, and provide the hypothalamus and the anterior pituitary with a constant flow of information regarding this crucial bodily process.

The messages shuttling from hypothalamus to anterior pituitary to thyroid and back again constitute a feedback mechanism that helps to regulate the amount of heat produced in our bodies, their cholesterol level, heart rate, respiration and blood pressure. The thyroid hormone acts as a catalyst for all these activities by burning more cellular energy.

A person whose thyroid is over-active becomes nervous, excitable, irritable and apprehensive—traits that are apparent in the Mercurial type. In extreme cases it also causes muscular tremors. Under-activity of the thyroid, on the other hand, makes people lethargic, cools the body and starves the cells of energy. Because of these wide-ranging effects, the balanced operation of the thyroid is essential to human activity.

The Anterior Pituitary and the Saturn Type

In this scheme of endocrine types Saturn is ruled by the anterior pituitary; the so-called *master gland*. It develops alongside the posterior pituitary. Dominating several of the other glands, the anterior pituitary is of utmost importance in the activity of the entire endocrine system.

The anterior pituitary directly stimulates the thyroid, adrenals and ovaries. It indirectly regulates growth, accelerates digestion and colors the skin. It is located at the base of the brain, in front of (anterior to) the posterior pituitary, through which it is connected to the hypothalamus.

Its own hormones contribute to the production of estrogen and progesterone, the sex hormones of the reproductive system. Although it is tied to Saturn, the most masculine body type, it seems to have at least as many maternal qualities as does the posterior part, which is connected to Jovial. One of its hormones—prolactin—helps women's breasts develop when pregnant, and also helps them give milk when nursing.

Over-activity of the anterior pituitary in childhood enlarges people into giants; under-activity of the gland creates dwarfs. In adults an oversupply of some of its hormones exaggerates the growth of the body's long bones and creates a condition known as acromegaly.

The Adrenals and the Martial Type

Mars is linked to the adrenals, a pair of glands atop the kidneys that rules almost as many of our functions as the anterior pituitary rules. Divided into two distinct spheres, the adrenals react in complex ways to stimuli from many different sources. Together they spawn more than 30 hormones that affect both the levels of sodium and potassium in the kidneys and the levels of fats and proteins in the liver. Some adrenal hormones modify the burning of carbohydrates. Others, like the sex hormones oestrogen and androgen, influence the reproductive system.

The adrenal cortex is the outer portion of the adrenals. Adrenal steroids produced here are called on by the anterior pituitary and the hypothalamus, which are constantly monitoring the level of corticosteroids in the blood. A change in this level causes the anterior pituitary to release hormones that in turn stimulate the adrenals to produce other hormones that correct the imbalance.

This is another example of the closed-loop, self-regulating nature of the endocrine system, in which glands communicate and interact with each other through complimentary chemical sensitivities. It is a process that plays a key part in regulating the levels of sodium and potassium, both of which are vital elements in maintaining the electrolytic stability of the body's fluids.

Under-activity of the adrenal cortex, which may allow the level of glucocorticoids in the system to drop, results in Addison's disease. This life-threatening condition weakens the body, causes fatigue, weight loss and anemia, and intensifies the pigmentation of the skin.

Over-activity is equally devastating, as a lack of potassium can make muscles shake, turn the complexion florid, deprive one of protein and raise the level of blood sugar. An excess production of glucocorticoids gives rise to Cushing's syndrome, which leads to a thinning of the skin that makes one bruise easily; it can also produce obesity. Over-activity of the adrenal cortex can afflict women with a grotesque virilism in which both male sex characteristics and male secondary sex organs are exaggerated far beyond normal.

The inner part of the adrenals is the medulla which, unlike the cortex, is controlled by the sympathetic nervous system. Through another complex process the adrenal medulla passes its messages to the hypothalamus, and in doing so bypasses the anterior pituitary. Instead, these messages travel through the medulla oblongata, one of the brain's most primitive parts. One of this gland's chief tasks is to stimulate the manufacture of epinephrine, or adrenaline. The adrenal medulla thus becomes associated with the 'fight-or-flight' effects of adrenaline, a hormone that is an essential part of the nervous system's response to stress.

Strong emotions, a pounding heart, blood flowing through muscles, climbing blood pressure and the burning of sugar for energy also cause the release of this potent hormone. Adrenaline prolongs the intensity of these functions by many of its effects; it constricts the smooth muscles of the skin, dilates the pupils, tightens the abdominal muscles and blood vessels, increases the air available to the body by relaxing the bronchioles in the windpipe, contracts the sphincter and ureter, mobilizes the fuel in muscles and liver, increases the sugar level and thereby the available energy carried by the blood and generally stimulates our entire metabolism. Adrenaline brings the body and its systems to a high pitch, prepared for immediate action.

The approach of combat can produce all these physiological changes, and so can the tremble of fear. Both are instinctive and automatic and both are necessary for survival. By catapulting us into violence or fear, the adrenals demonstrate the very dramatic changes that are brought about by their hormone, adrenaline.

The Posterior Pituitary and the Jovial Type

The pituitary gland lies deep in the recesses of the brain and develops in two distinct directions until, in adults, it becomes a two-lobed gland. While still an embryo, the anterior part grows upward from the roof of the primitive mouth cavity. The posterior part is created from tissue growing up from the floor of the primitive brain, and eventually connects to the adult brain by way of the pituitary stalk.

Although the posterior pituitary secretes two chief hormones it produces neither of them. This gland, coupled to the Jovial type, is in one sense an elementary part of the hypothalamus. The hormones the hypothalamus produces are passed to the posterior pituitary for release into the body. One of these hormones has an effect on the fluid balance in the body; the other is oxytocin, which is partly responsible for women's birth contractions, and for the production of milk in nursing mothers.

While our knowledge of the posterior pituitary is very incomplete, we do know that it plays a variety of roles. It acts not only as an endocrine gland, but also as an integral part of the hypothalamus by releasing the antidiuretic hormone, which is made in the hypothalamus, into the body.

The antidiuretic hormone performs a crucial service by helping to keep the body's internal environment in balance. This balance—or equilibrium—is called *homeostasis*. It includes the body's temperature, appetite and thirst, its electrolytic balance and its acid-base balance. It also includes the body's overall level of energy. By bringing balance to the body's homeostasis, the posterior pituitary helps to ensure man's survival.

The Thymus, Gland of Solar Body Type

The thymus, a small gland composed of a mass of white blood cells, is located in the upper chest under the breastbone. It is associated with the Solar type. This gland grows throughout childhood but starts to shrink after puberty. It produces some hormone-like substances that affect the immune system's development, and it influences the functioning of the immune system.

The thymus also processes white blood cells (or lymphocytes) which provide one of the body's basic defenses against foreign invasion. Lymphocytes excite other cells of the immune system to produce the antibodies that the body summons to combat alien infestation and infection. An imbalance in any of this work can rout the body's defenses and make it susceptible to disease.

The Sex Organs

The sex organs—men's testes and women's ovaries—are related to Uranus, a planet that doesn't represent a specific type in the scheme of body types. Instead, it seems to stand for the creative and procreative functions in all people. But the sex organs also have a hand in one part of the endocrine system's control of body functions. These glands produce sex hormones that govern the development of secondary sex organs and secondary sex characteristics. The anterior pituitary and the hypothalamus dominate the work of the testes and the ovaries.

A man's secondary sex organs are those organs that produce and transport spermatozoa, including the penis. The hormones that control these organs also determine the quality of his secondary sex characteristics; the deepness of his voice, the amount of his pubic and body hair and the general shape and character to his body that make it male.

Women's ovaries produce the hormones that channel the development of their secondary sex organs. These hormones influence the organs that produce and deliver the eggs to be fertilized, and the vagina. They also spur the changes in a woman's breasts that are necessary for her to feed her young. Normal breast development, the amount of a woman's body hair and the typical proportions and rounded curves of the female body are all secondary sex characteristics whose character is dictated by these same hormones.

The Pineal Body

The last endocrine gland we will look at is the pineal body. This small cone-shaped gland is buried deep in the brain, midway between the temples and centered directly behind the eyes. The theory of types relates the pineal gland to Neptune, another planet that lacks any connection to a specific type. Neptune supplies us instead with a symbol of a higher type of man, one in whom a new function operates.

Despite a good deal of investigation, the pineal remains largely unknown. Researchers suspect that it reacts to the amount of light our eyes take in. They think that it produces melatonin—a hormone somehow involved with the menstrual cycle—which may also inhibit the work of the ovaries.

In some lower animals the pineal develops into an eye-like structure called the pineal eye. Partly because of this evidence it is sometimes thought to be the remnant of a primitive sense organ. But in many mystic sciences the pineal gland is seen as the seed of man's higher functions, those that are only potential in normal life. These functions are thought to be connected to some *third eye*; a new, rather than a vestigial, organ. What these higher faculties may be, and how the pineal affects them, are questions closed to scientific explanation for the time being.

The work of the pineal gland remains as mysterious as its effects are elusive. It may be, as Rene Descartes said, the organ of 'common sense.' But it also hints that there is a possibility for the body to develop new ways to control what we might call its potential *higher* abilities.

The pineal gland also represents a new possibility for man—his chance to develop new, and higher, psychic functions. What these functions would be we can only guess, as we can only guess what they would mean for the person who had managed to acquire them.

Bibliography

Anthony, Catherine Parker and Gary A. Thibodeau. *Structure and Function of the Body*. 7th ed. St. Louis: Times Mirror/Mosby College Publishing, 1984.

Benham, William G. *The Benham Book of Palmistry: A Practical Treatise on the Laws of Scientific Hand Reading*. North Hollywood: Newcastle Publishing, 1988.

Berman, Louis. *The Glands Regulating Personality*. New York: 1929.

Boardman, John. *The Parthenon and Its Sculptures*. Austin: University of Texas Press, 1985.

Bulfinch, Thomas. *Bulfinch's Mythology*. New York: Thomas Y. Crowell Company, n.d.

Burton, Robert Earl. *Self-Remembering*. New York: Globe Press Books, 1991.

Christeaan, Aaron, J.P. Van Hulle, and M.C. Clark. *Michael, The Basic Teachings*. Orinda, California: Affinity Press, 1988.

Clark, Kenneth. *The Nude*. Princeton: Princeton University Press, 1972.

Collin, Rodney. *The Theory of Celestial Influence*. New York: Samuel Weiser Inc., 1971.

——. *The Theory of Eternal Life*. Boulder: Shambhala, 1984.

Concise Columbia Encyclopedia, The. New York: Avon (published by arrangement with Columbia University Press), 1983.

Flaceliere, Robert. *A Literary History of Greece.* Translated by Douglas Garman. Chicago: Aldine Publishing Company, 1964.

Goethe, Johann Wolfgang von. *Elective Affinities.* Translated by R.J. Hollingdale. Middlesex, England: Penguin Books, 1983.

Groenewegen-Frankfort, H.A., and Bernard Ashmole. *Art of the Ancient World.* New York: Harry N. Abrams, Inc., n.d.

Gurdjieff, George. *Meetings with Remarkable Men.* New York: E.P. Dutton & Company, Inc., 1963.

———. *Views from the Real World.* New York: E.P. Dutton, 1975.

Hammond, N.G.L., and H.H. Scullard, eds. *The Oxford Classical Dictionary.* 2d ed. Oxford: Clarendon Press, 1977.

Hinnells, John R., ed. *The Penguin Dictionary of Religions.* Middlesex, England: Penguin Books, 1984.

The Holy Bible. Cambridge: The Cambridge University Press, n.d.

Kitto, H.D.F. *The Greeks.* Middlesex, England: Penguin Books, 1979.

Keyes, Margaret Frings. *Emotions and the Enneagram.* Muir Beach, California: Molysdatur Publications, 1992.

Liggett, John. *The Human Face.* New York: Stein and Day, 1974.

McNaught, Ann B., and Robin Callander. *Illustrated Physiology.* 4th ed. New York: Churchill Livingstone, 1983.

Metzner, Ralph. *Know Your Type: Maps of Identity.* Garden City, New York: Anchor Books, 1979.

Moore, Patrick, and Garry Hunt. *Atlas of the Solar System.* Chicago: Rand McNally & Company, 1984.

Morris, Richard. *Time's Arrows-Scientific Attitudes Toward Time.* New York: Simon and Schuster, 1985.

Ouspensky, P.D. *The Fourth Way.* New York: Vintage Books, 1971.

———. *A New Model of the Universe*. New York: Vintage Books, 1971.

———. *The Psychology of Man's Possible Evolution*. New York: Vintage Books, 1974.

———. *In Search of the Miraculous*. New York: Harcourt Brace Jovanovich, Inc., 1977.

———. *Tertium Organum*. Translated by Nicholas Bessaraboff and Claude Bragdon. New York: Alfred A. Knopf, 1968.

Ovid. *The Metamorphoses*. Translated by Horace Gregory. New York: The New American Library, 1964.

Palmer, Helen. *The Enneagram*. San Francisco: Harper and Row, 1988.

Plutarch. *The Lives of the Noble Grecians and Romans*. Translated by John Dryden. New York: The Modern Library, n.d.

Redgrove, H. Stanley. *Alchemy: Ancient and Modern*. 2d ed. New Hyde Park, New York: University Books, Inc., 1969.

Reyner, J.H. *The Diary of a Modern Alchemist*. London: Neville Spearman, 1974.

Saltus, Carol. *Bodyscopes: Your Guide to How Body Structure Reveals the Secrets of Personality*. New York: Bantam Books, 1986.

Spence, Lewis. *An Encyclopedia of Occultism*. New Hyde Park, New York: University Books, Inc., 1968.

Stassinopoulos, Arianna, and Roloff Beny. *The Gods of Greece*. London: Weidenfeld & Nicolson, 1983.

Wagner, Carl E. Jr. *Characterology, The Art & Science of Character Analysis*. York Beach, Maine: Samuel Weiser, 1986.

Other Books of Interest

The Training of the Zen Buddhist Monk
by D. T. Suzuki. This is perhaps the best introduction to Zen and the life of the Zen monk. Forty-three illustrations by the monk Zenchu Sato depict many common practices in the life of the monks. 1991. 176 pages, 43 illustrations. Softcover, $9.95.

Self Remembering
by Robert Earl Burton. In talks to his students a modern teacher of the Fourth Way shows how to use the ancient practice of self-remembering to fully penetrate the elusive present. 1993. 232 pages. Softcover, $15.00.

Letters from Nowhere
A World-Renowned Esotericist Recounts His Spiritual Journeys
by Raymond Bernard. From the Druzes of Lebanon to Rosicrucian mysticism, from India's secret ashrams to the Grand Lamas of Tibet, Raymond Bernard takes us on a journey of discovery in which the inner world is the true destination. A CIRCES Book, translated by Theodore J. Nottingham. 1992. 204 pages, softcover, $14.95.

Available at fine bookstores, or order direct from the publisher. To order send check or money order along with $2.50 per item for shipping to:
Joel Friedlander, *publisher*
Post Office Box 552
Yorktown, NY 10598.